A fabulous tr̶ guide to the glo̶ *Abbey's* filming, t̶ II listed cottage extension *and* hilarious showbiz stories thrown into the mix – naturally all in a day's work for a comedy actress! This book will have you in fits of laughter!

Rowena Perkins
– Cotswold TV

Another passionate love note to the Cotswolds and a great romp, by turns, funny, touching, entertaining, informative and with glorious colour photographs of the Cotswolds and *Downton Abbey's* film locations and celebrities.

Diz has done it again with a new laugh-out-loud, good life, foodie, meet the *Downton Abbey* celebrities, remodel a cottage, explore the idyllic Cotswolds, fun read.

– Wanda Ventham
Actress and Cotswolds resident,
Absolutely Fabulous: The Movie, Sherlock, Dr Who

More Cotswolds Memoirs is as enchanting as Diz White's earlier book *Cotswolds Memoir* and again, although it is hard to fathom how building an addition onto a cottage would make for an exciting story, here is another fun-filled adventure. The reader is beguiled by Diz's story, which comes from the heart. There is an underlying depth to this author's warm, friendly and, on many occasions, hilariously funny writing.

– William Greenleaf
Greenleaf Literary Magazine

More Cotswolds Memoirs

Creating the Perfect Cottage and
Discovering Downton Abbey in the Cotswolds

by

Diz White

More Cotswolds Memoirs
Creating the Perfect Cottage and Discovering Downton Abbey in The Cotswolds

by
Diz White

ISBN: 978-0-9571162-4-5

Published by Larrabee Libraries, a Division of Larrabee Industries, in conjunction with Writersworld. This book is produced entirely in the UK, is available to order from most book shops in the United Kingdom, and is globally available via UK-based Internet book retailers and www.amazon.com.

Copy edited by Ian Large

Cover design by Randall Montgomery and Jag Lall

Additional photos by James Wildman: www.jameswildman.co.uk

WRITERSWORLD
2 Bear Close Flats, Bear Close, Woodstock,
Oxfordshire, OX20 1JX, England

☎ 01993 812500
☎ +44 1993 812500

www.writersworld.co.uk

The text pages of this book are produced via an independent certification process that ensures the trees from which the paper is produced come from well-managed sources that exclude the risk of using illegally logged timber while leaving options to use post-consumer recycled paper as well.

Contents

Other Books by this Author vi
About the Author vii
An Introduction ix

One   A LITTLE BIT OF HEAVEN
              Down Ampney, Fairford, Newbridge 1

Two   WISTERIA COTTAGE
              Minchinhampton, Uley, Nympsfield 15

Three DOWNTON ABBEY DISCOVERED
              Bampton, Little Rissington, Minster Lovell 31

Four   RUSTY THE IRON AGE MAN
              Chipping Campden, Bourton on the Hill, Ebrington 46

Five   A LOT MORE OF DOWNTON
              Swinbrook, Cogges, Great Coxwell 62

Six   PLAYING THE WAITING GAME
              Church Enstone, Neat Enstone, Fulwell 99

Seven TEA IN THE BALLROOM
              Northleach, Yanworth, Winchcombe 117

Eight SAVING THE PIGGERY
              Faringdon, Stanton Harcourt, Standlake 130

Nine   FOODIE DELIGHTS
              Stroud, Duntisbourne Abbots, Frampton Mansell 141

Ten   COTSWOLD BLISS
              Warwick, Broughton, Beveston 150

Cotswolds Visitor Guide – *historic sites, attractions,*
                            restaurants, open gardens,
                            conservation, information 167
Resource Guide 183
Acknowledgements 185
Index 186

Other Books by this Author

Cotswolds Memoir*: Discovering a Beautiful Region of Britain on a Quest to Buy a 17th Century Cottage* (Larrabee Libraries)
Haunted Cotswolds (The History Press)
Haunted Cheltenham (The History Press)
The Comedy Group Book (Smith and Kraus)
El Grande de Coca-Cola (Samuel French Play scripts)
Bullshot Crummond (Samuel French Play scripts)
Footlight Frenzy (Samuel French Play scripts)

Other Media by this Author

DVD – *GHOSTS OF GREAT BRITAIN COLLECTION* – *Haunted Cotswolds* (Available on Amazon)

MOVIE – now in DVD — *BULLSHOT* (HandMade Films) (Available on Amazon)

Every effort has been made to ensure that the facts in this book are accurate. However, the author and publishers cannot accept responsibility for any loss, injury or inconvenience however caused. Some names, locations and events have been changed to protect anonymity.

A portion of the proceeds of this book will be donated to conservation institutions that benefit the Cotswolds region. This region is a designated AONB (Area of Outstanding Natural Beauty), and is overseen by the Cotswolds Conservation Board.

About the Author

British-born Diz White divides her time between the Cotswolds and Hollywood where she pursues a career as an actress, comedy writer and producer for films and television. Her acting work ranges from *Star Trek: Next Generation* to *Bullshot* the comedy movie, now a cult hit, in which she starred and co-wrote for HandMade Films. Diz received a New York Critics' *Drama Desk Award* for her role in *El Grande de Coca-Cola* and this show, which she also co-wrote, was subsequently filmed as a comedy special for HBO.

Diz is the author of *Cotswolds Memoir: Discovering a Beautiful Region of Britain on a Quest to Buy a 17th Century Cottage* (Larrabee Libraries) and also *Haunted Cotswolds* and *Haunted Cheltenham*, (both published by The History Press). Diz authored three plays for Samuel French Playscripts: *El Grande de Coca-Cola, Bullshot Crummond* and *Footlight Frenzy*.

This author is currently developing a feature film, adapted from her book, *Cotswolds Memoir*, and working on a non-fiction book about the Cotswolds.

Diz really enjoys hearing from her readers and can be reached through her website www.dizwhite.com.

An Introduction

Join me as I continue the journey which began in my last book *Cotswolds Memoirs* with a quest to buy a 17th century cottage. An acting career had taken me from England to the USA where I'd married an American and settled in. Eventually, however, my roots began to pull me back to England, re-awakening my dream of owning a cottage in the Cotswolds.

Together with my husband Randy I bought 17th century Wisteria Cottage and decided some renovation would be needed to make it perfect. However, I had no idea that carrying out these alterations would lead to yet another roller-coaster, laughter-filled ride packed with as many highs, heartbreaks and cliff-hangers as my earlier one and even more fun.

This adventure encompasses all my passions; I'm a foodie, a history buff, a nature lover and love to laugh. I'm also a looky-loo (I can't get enough of old houses and fantasising about how I would remodel them).

Although *More Cotswolds Memoirs* can be read independently, many of the same quirky, amusing characters from *Cotswolds Memoir* reappear to enhance the fun. In this sojourn I roam across the countryside in search of reclaimed oak floorboards, slate roof tiles, Victorian door handles and just the right pub for lunch. I visit Roman settlements, ancient villages, Domesday churches, open gardens, antique emporiums, nature hikes, and along the way discover the *Downton Abbey* film locations in the Cotswolds, delve into their history and meet celebrities from the series.

I contend with a collapsing piggery during the renovation, fend off marauding cows, and risk life and limb for the best bargains at the Church Westcote fête. I sup on Barnsley lamb, Old Spot pork and experience every 'good life' delight on offer.

Scrambling between my frenetic Hollywood career and the Cotswolds, I take every showbiz job, during which I often descend the ladder of success in order to fund the cottage renovation.

My love for my Cotswold community deepens when many in the village pitch in to help after obstacles threaten to overwhelm me.

By acquiring an education in renovation and building regulations I am able to offer valuable practical advice and ingenious solutions to those on the same journey.

Creating the perfect cottage led to further exploration of off-the-beaten-track Cotswolds. There is more to enjoy in this region than the same chocolate box villages, lovely as they are, that visitors are routinely directed towards.

My Visitor Guide at the end of this narrative focuses on much that is overlooked in the usual tourist information with suggestions of the best Cotswolds attractions.

What could be more idyllic than hearing the chimes of an ancient church from a bench outside a rustic country pub with matchless views overlooking the Golden Valley by Stroud or a stroll through a peaceful village, its medieval, honey-hued cottages cuddling each other higgledy-piggledy, in all their wonky glory, a riot of honeysuckle festooning their fronts. Writing my Cotswolds books has been a joy and an added bonus during the books' research and publicity has been to visit places and meet people I would never otherwise have known, leading to some wonderful lasting friendships.

My passion for the Cotswolds extends to its conservation and at the end of this narrative there is a Conservation Guide along with a Resource Guide containing information for listed property owners and other useful material.

Should the reader decide to tag along, perhaps you'll join me for afternoon tea on the lawn of Wisteria Cottage. My husband, most likely, will be strumming his ukulele and crooning to the lilt of *Isn't It Romantic* and I'll be singing along, totally happy in my Cotswold bliss.

Diz White

Kiftsgate Court Garden

Photographs
by Randall Montgomery
www.montgomeryfoto.com
(unless otherwise credited)

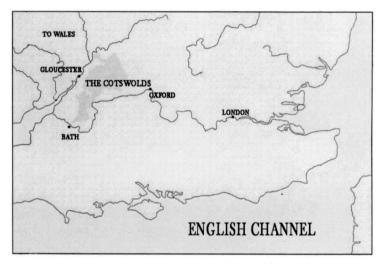

The Cotswolds

Owlpen Manor

For my husband Randall with love,
my mother Josephine Ashley, the poet
and my dear family

One

A LITTLE BIT OF HEAVEN
Down Ampney, Fairford, Newbridge

"Look out! It's going to break!" I yelled to my husband as a dozen or so cows pushed up against the single strand of wire separating our garden from the Cotswold meadow where they grazed. The wire was stretched so tight that it was about to snap, but the cows continued to jostle each other and inch forward. They had no choice as they were being shouldered from behind by a massive, curly-headed bull.

"Quick, shoo them away – if they get in they'll ruin the plants and fall in the pond!" I screamed.

"I'm trying!" my husband Randy yelled back as he frantically waved his arms at the herd.

I was terrified that the wire would snap and the cows would easily climb over the low stone wall underneath it. There was no proper fence so that the lovely field view could be seen from the garden and up until now it had not been a problem.

On a number of occasions I'd enjoyed watching the cows as I relaxed in a lawn chair and took tea on the terrace. They would often get curious and politely put their heads over the one strand of wire as they appeared to join in the conversation. I would stroke their velvet noses as I fed them sticks of celery, but today was an alarmingly different story.

"It's April, they must have Spring fever!" Randy shouted. It was time for desperate measures. My husband ran straight at the cows, this time wildly waving a rake. This made no impression on them at all and they surged forward again, the wire twanging with the strain.

We both yelled and waved our arms. They didn't blink. Randy was all for climbing over into the meadow and pushing the cows away, but I stopped him and pointed out the potential danger of the bull, who was looking more agitated by the second.

"What can I do? We've got to save our plants," Randy shouted desperately.

Suddenly a mad idea popped into my head.

"Sing to them,"

"What? Why?"

"I read about it somewhere, try it," I replied.

"What shall I sing?"

Remembering that my husband had performed in shows in New York I made a suggestion.

"Something loud from a Broadway musical."

Randy took a deep breath and bellowed:

"Willkommen! Bienvenue! Welcome! Im Cabaret, Au Cabaret, To Cabaret!"

Nothing changed.

Next, becoming slightly unhinged, Randy added some of Cabaret choreographer Bob Fosse's dancing to his rendition of the song. My husband has a lovely singing voice but a dancer he is not. With his hands spread open at hip level he performed a particularly deranged version of Fosse's signature jerky movements in double quick time to the ringing tones of:

"Meine Damen und Herren – Mes dames et Messieurs."

The effect was astonishing.

The cows froze in open-jawed amazement and then, appearing to have been struck by lightning, turned as one and galloped away across the meadow, the bull lumbering after them. Their thundering hooves were reminiscent of a stampede in a Western movie.

"No wonder I couldn't get cast in musicals," said Randy. "When I danced at auditions that was exactly the same reaction I got from casting directors."

We sighed with relief as the danger was over. Who else can say that their garden plants were saved from destruction by the inspiration of Liza Minelli and Joel Grey? A couple of neighbours walking in the meadow with their dog had witnessed the whole scene and were convulsed with laughter.

"Come join the COWbaret!" we yelled and finished the song and dance for them.

"Willkommen! Bienvenue! Welcome! Im Cabaret. Au Cabaret. To Cowbaret!"

This was all happening in the garden of my little piece of heaven in the Cotswolds – Wisteria Cottage. My husband and I were now happily nestled there – living the dream of owning a 17th century Cotswold home. It had been a roller coaster ride to reach my goal of buying this beautiful place after many hilarious adventures, which I describe in my last book, *Cotswolds Memoir: Discovering a Beautiful Region of Britain on a Quest to Buy a 17th Century Cottage.* Everything was perfect. Well, almost perfect – the problem was we didn't quite fit into Wisteria Cottage – the big drawback was the living room which was the size of a postage stamp.

In order to put this right I was about to embark on my next big adventure – building an extension that would include a living room, a small study and a bathroom. As Wisteria Cottage was Grade II listed this wasn't going to be as straightforward as ordinary building work.

We had bought one of Britain's 450,000 listed buildings and now owned a cottage that was part of the national heritage. Grade II indicates the building is of 'special interest', Grade II* is more than 'special interest' and Grade I of 'exceptional interest'. All need planning permission from the local council before any alterations are to be made. It was dawning on me slowly how complicated building this extension could possibly become.

I am an English-born actress and a writer and together with my American husband, Randy, divide my time between Hollywood and the Cotswolds. After being based in America for a number of years, an increasing craving for Yorkshire pudding had signalled that my roots were tugging me back to my homeland. When this surfeit of puddings was threatening to prevent me from fitting through doors I tried to quell my homesickness by watching lots of English movies instead. But this failed to do the trick and I decided that in order to feel happy I needed to spend some significant time in England. Subsequently, my husband and I rented holiday accommodation for a few weeks for several summers in the Cotswolds and eventually this convinced me that the only lasting cure for my homesickness was to actually own my own 17th century cottage. I achieved my goal, Randy and I completed on the purchase and my long-held dream of owning a cottage came true. We celebrated with a big housewarming party, which despite my best efforts somehow turned into something of a hilarious Buster Keaton farce.

I imagined that once I had overcome the Herculean challenge of buying and moving into Wisteria Cottage, life would settle into a serene rhythm of gentle days – with lots of time spent lazily reading books in the garden, in between writing sessions, as the bees buzzed, followed by tea on the terrace every afternoon. This illusion had been shattered almost immediately with the narrowly averted frisky cow invasion. Now I was coming to the realization that together with all the plans and arrangements I had in mind and the building work coming up for the extension, which no doubt would present some difficulties, I was most likely in for yet another unpredictable adventure. But, if it was going to be as much fun as the last one, I decided, then bring it on.

After finally moving into lovely Wisteria Cottage, only a short time passed before I had to return to work in Hollywood to help finance the renovation. Both of us worked hard and saved every penny. The months had finally rolled around and now it was Spring again. The Hollywood studios mostly close for hiatus between June and August. This meant that I could split my time and spend the winter months in Hollywood pursuing my career as an actress and vocal artiste and then return to the Cotswolds in the Summer and my other career as a book author. Although I have authored books and plays about other subjects, writing about the fascinating history, architecture and good life of the Cotswolds is the topic that gives me the most joy. Carrying out research for my books is a pure delight as I get to explore this lovely area, with its limitless beauty and incredibly interesting history.

We had managed to leave Hollywood early and in the first week of April here I was, back luxuriating in Cotswold bliss with the whole glorious English Spring and Summer stretching ahead of me. It felt so good to be back in our Cotswold cottage even though there was work to be done. There had been sunny weather before we arrived in England, bringing all the plants along quickly, and now everything was beginning to burst into bloom. A tall holly tree on our land was draped in an avalanche of white *clematis Montana*, swathed like a wedding veil entwining the foliage from the crown down to the lowest branches with its delicate blossoms. A drift of daffodils cast a yellow glow under the apple tree. A pair of doves was building a nest at eye level in a honeysuckle vine in the garden and we watched Mama Dove's progress as she and her partner busily set to work.

Just after we arrived, and still suffering from jet lag, I awoke very early one morning and was amazed to see a thick mist enveloping the field view. Instead of the usual vista of fields, trees and hedges, visibility was reduced to just a few yards beyond the dry stone wall that borders our land. I took my tea outside and looked in awe as the mist began to slowly swirl, making fantastic shapes as it curled around the edges of trees and lifted a little off the ground. After a few moments a lowing sound heralded a cow, wreathed in mist, emerging like a sepia painting from another era. Cotswold cows are among my favourite creatures and this one was enhanced even more by the soft focus treatment of the gently dissolving background.

As more cows were gradually revealed Randy joined me and, grabbing his camera, captured these images before the mist was dissolved by the warm sun. Eventually the day evolved into a glorious scorcher, but I'll never forget those magical, early morning moments when my lovely Cotswold cows materialised out of the mist like a painting by Turner.

Only a couple of days earlier, the farmer had mowed this field after it had grown waist high with grass over the winter months. No doubt the gorgeous scent of the newly-cut Spring grass had helped to make the cows frisky, thus putting our garden into jeopardy, before it was saved by Randy's cow-scaring dance.

The weather was wonderful with the promise of sunny days for the foreseeable future. Randy decided that our jet lag would be helped by some good food. So that evening we invited our friends Sandra and Jim, fellow actors from the next village, over for dinner. This couple had helped us find our cottage, giving us an amazing number of tips, and we toasted them with a crisp Champagne the moment they arrived. Randy already had a leg of Cotswold lamb slowly turning on the rotisserie of the barbeque, having tucked fresh rosemary and plenty of garlic into small slits in the meat. We sipped Champagne as we ate hors d'oeuvres of crudité with a tzatziki dip.

The lamb wafted a delicious scent across the terrace as I made a salad of tomato, red onion and basil, slathered with olive oil, while we chatted. I added a small amount of freshly grated ginger then drizzled the salad with aged balsamic glaze vinegar.

I had roasted sweet potatoes earlier with their skins left on and afterwards split them half open. I scooped out a portion of the sweet potato pulp and mixed it with strained Greek yogurt and finely grated fresh horseradish. Next, I put the mixture back into the scooped-out sweet potatoes and finished off with a garnish of fresh chopped chives and grated Parmesan cheese.

It was just warm enough, with our jackets on, to sit out on the terrace for dinner and as we ate we caught up on all the village news with Sandra and Jim.

Next, we chatted about building our extension. As our cottage was listed we knew that we would have to get planning permission from the local council but we had no idea how to go about it.

"We can recommend an architectural planner; he'll sort all of that out for you and make the application to the council. I'll email his contact info tomorrow," said Jim, confidently.

"Do you know for sure that he is good? I've read that getting permission on listed buildings is quite tricky," I asked.

"Yvonne and Bob used him and they were very happy. Their place isn't listed but I'm sure he covers it all. They said his fee was very reasonable. They did quite a bit of research before they chose him and said he was even better than an architect because he was also trained to plan space with an eye to interior design too."

"Yes," said Sandy, "architects can sometimes make things look so industrial and cold."

"Oh," I replied, "I don't want that – we are going for the traditional cottage look."

"Well as this chap is an architectural planner it sounds like he is one for you," said Jim.

"You steered us right before," replied Randy, indicating Wisteria Cottage sitting cosily across the terrace. "We wouldn't be here without your tips. Seems like we need to look no further."

We all clinked our glasses as we toasted Jim and Sandy and thanked them again. Next, Randy passed me another delectable slice of roast lamb, infused with garlic and rosemary and all was right with the world. We finished our meal and marvelled at the gorgeous sunset which spread itself above our field view in a dazzling array of pinks and reds.

We made our appointment with the architectural planner, who I shall call Mr T, and a few days later set off for an initial meeting with him at his office. We departed early as we had been invited to lunch by Brigadier Murgatroyd and his wife, the Honourable Mrs Murgatroyd. Randy and I had met this elderly aristocratic couple, the owners of a rambling manor house and almost the entire hamlet that surrounded it, when we stayed in Stable Cottage, one of their holiday rentals, before buying Wisteria Cottage. It was during my stay in Stable Cottage that my love affair with the Cotswolds had begun and I was longing to squeeze in as much exploring as I could, so with that in mind, we stopped off for a quick tour of the small village of Down Ampney on the way.

This pretty, medium-sized village in the county of Gloucestershire is about five miles south-east of Cirencester and is well known for its historic All Saint's Church. Although much of this church was rebuilt in Victorian times, it was founded by the Knights Templar in 1265 and features fascinating effigies of Sir Nicholas de Valers, a knight who is thought to have founded the church. This chap is ready for battle clad in full armour, shown drawing his sword as he reclines on a lion. Next to him is an effigy of his wife. After a tour of the church I wanted to see the lovely manor house too, but there wasn't time. On our way out of the village as we drove on past the pretty 17th Century cottages, I vowed to spend more time in Down Ampney another day.

A short time later the Murgatroyd's manor house appeared through the trees as we motored down their long winding drive. This house must have originally been built in the late 1700s and apparently a new wing had been added every fifty years or so. No effort seemed to have been made with the additional construction to keep to the original design and the subsequent collage of architectural styles gave a haphazard look to its overall appearance. The brigadier had come from a long line of army officers and his wife was the younger daughter of a baron. He was very much the feudal country squire of his small village. He knew his place and expected everyone who lived there to know theirs. The Murgatroyds owned the land of the whole surrounding area, which included their manor house, the small church nearby, the old school house, various outbuildings including stables, barns, a row of worker's cottages and a couple of working farms.

Being in their company was a little like stepping back a hundred years. Hilariously batty as they could be at times, we had come to realise that underneath all this eccentricity ran a font of wisdom and we came to value their sage advice. Time spent in their holiday cottage had greatly enhanced our vacations and invitations to have drinks with them in their sprawling manor had provided a fascinating glimpse into an aristocratic way of life that was fast disappearing. Their quirky personalities and frequent departures from logic often made it hard for us to keep a straight face but gradually over the course of several summers we had grown very fond of them.

"Hello, Brigadier Murgatroyd, how are you?" I asked as we were shown into the drawing room by an ancient butler.

"Well my doctors tell me I've got a dicky ticker and my brain is turning into a sponge, but what do they know? Wait a minute, who are you?"

"We're the Montgomerys," I said.

"Oh, do I know you?"

"Yes, we rented one of your cottages for several summers."

"What's your line of work?"

"We're actors," I replied.

"No, no," said the Brigadier, "what do you do for a living?"

Randy replied. "That is what we do for a living, we're actors, we work in films and television and perform in cartoons and do impressions."

Mrs Murgatroyd overheard this last exchange as she entered the drawing room.

"Oh Harold," she said addressing the Brigadier, "surely you remember the Montgomerys, they rented Stable Cottage from us before they bought Wisteria Cottage."

Harold stared blankly at us as Mrs Murgatroyd continued.

"They are the ones who do funny voices."

"Yes," I said, helpfully.

"Randy's very good at them. He imitates all the Presidents from Obama right back to Ronald Reagan." With that Randy imitated Ronald Reagan's voice.

"Hello my fellow Americans. Mommy and I are pleased to meet you."

Brigadier Murgatroyd was completely taken aback by hearing a different voice coming out of Randy.

"What on earth are you playing at?" he asked.

"He's doing Ronald Reagan," I replied.

"You know, the President" added Randy

"Do we know the President?" said Mrs Murgatroyd, mistaking Randy's statement for a question.

"No. Not personally." She continued answering her own question. "We were never introduced. Harold, they know Ronald Reagan."

"No, I don't know him, I just imitate his voice," said Randy.

Mrs Murgatroyd, looking puzzled, asked "Why? Has he got laryngitis?"

"No", I said, "it's called voice matching. We imitate an actor's voice and replace any sound takes that may have been spoiled."

Mrs Murgatroyd's expression of amazement was a sight to behold as she asked,"And you do this for a living?"

A change of subject seemed a good idea right then. Desperately glancing around the drawing room looking for a new topic, before I laughed out loud, I pointed to a large oil painting hanging in an alcove. It portrayed an alarmingly severe looking woman, dressed in some kind of Victorian era servant's uniform.

"Who is this lady?" I asked.

Mrs Murgatroyd replied. "That's Nanny Thompson – she was nanny to the family for over forty years. We had that painting of her hanging upstairs in the nursery but we had to take it down because it scared the children."

Conversation skidded to a halt as Randy and I sat silently chuckling, not daring to look at each other in case we completely lost control.

At this point, the ancient butler reappeared, holding a large silver salver at the centre of which were seven or eight tiny squares of bread covered in miniscule dabs of smoked salmon. He crossed the room excruciatingly slowly and, as he focused on circumnavigating the sofa to reach us, failed to keep the silver salver level. Its front end slowly drooped and we watched fascinated as the squares of bread slid down and teetered on the edge of the plate. The Murgatroyds must have noticed this but remained absolutely unmoved. By the time the decrepit butler did a repeat performance with four small glasses of pre-lunch sherry, saved only by everybody grabbing their glass at the last possible moment, well, we didn't know where to put ourselves.

After lunch, we told our hosts of our plan to build an extension. They both looked rather startled.

"Goodness me," said Mrs M. "I do hope you know what you are taking on. You'll have to get planning permission. Your cottage is listed, isn't it?"

"Yes," I replied, "the previous owners got planning permission from the council already but we do want some changes to their plans."

"You'll have to apply again in that case. If there is a different planning officer he could have a different opinion about your plans. It can all be very arbitrary. Have you had the new plans drawn up yet?" asked Mrs M.

"No, we are on our way to meet an architectural planner, this afternoon. In fact, look at the time – thanks so much for lunch – we'd better be off. We want to stop in Fairford on the way."

I had another stop planned on the way to our appointment as I had long wanted to stop in Fairford to see its star attraction, St. Mary's Church. Although not a 'chocolate box village' of the Cotswolds, Fairford has its own charm and its church, which was consecrated in 1497, is world-renowned for its fine stained glass windows.

This small town, about four miles from Lechlade on the River Coln, was made prosperous in the late medieval period by the Tames wool merchant family who built the church. Its medieval stained glass windows are the only ones to have remained intact from this period in the whole of Great Britain. And what fabulous windows they are. The sheer scale of them is extraordinarily impressive. The vibrant, jewel colours of the glass soaring up to the massively high oak-beamed rafters are breathtaking.

It is fortunate that these windows did not get ruined during the Civil War and Cromwell's rule which followed, when many other English churches had their stained glass destroyed. There are several theories concerning their survival. Traces of whitewash have been found on the glass indicating they may have been painted over during this time. Or some of the windows may have had the glass taken out and hidden until it was safe to restore them. Whatever the reason, these windows make a trip to Fairford well worth the trouble.

The artistry of Barnard Flower was employed by Henry VIII to glaze the windows and the skills of other French and English artists may also have contributed to this fine work. Randy and I were fascinated to discover that each window tells a story and there are 'hidden' portraits in the designs. One of the windows portrays the Queen of Sheba bringing gifts to King Solomon. Her Tudor clothing indicates that Queen Elizabeth of York may have been used as the model for this section of stained glass.

There are several other treasures here that make this church a must-see but my particular favourite is the wooden carvings known as misericords.

Monks were at one time required to stand as they sang in church but eventually they were allowed tip-up seats for the fatigued clerics to support themselves. These seats were called misericords from the Latin word for 'mercy'. Scenes were carved onto them which included all manner of fanciful depictions, including imaginary creatures, medieval folk tales, animals and foliage. The misericords in St. Mary's are beautifully carved and feature amusing scenes of a well-fed sleeping man, a dog stealing food from a cooking pot and a fox capturing a goose.

Next, we strolled around the town and discovered that Fairford was once a major coach stage on the London to Gloucester run, with the charming Bull Hotel coaching inn still serving a good lunch and a pint in its centre. There were a couple of interesting antique shops on the main street but we didn't have time to explore more before needing to hurry off to our appointment.

At the meeting Mr T listened as we described the extension we would need. We had brought the plans that had been drawn up several years ago for the previous owners, the survey that had been done and the council's planning permission. We pointed out that changes were needed from these plans. After studying them for a while Mr T said, with an air of complete confidence, "That shouldn't be a problem."

"Have you been able to get planning permission for a lot of listed properties like ours?" I asked.

"Not for listed properties so much but I've a lot of experience and the process is virtually the same whatever the age of the building. Don't worry, I'll fix it all up for you," he said, smiling.

When we told him our budget a cloud seemed to pass over his face and he looked thoughtful.

"Hmm... well I'll need to come over to look at your property and work up some figures before we talk too much about budget."

After we left I felt I needed to be near the river for some cool breezes as the weather had turned sultry and humid. We drove to the Thames and strolled along the towpath as we discussed Mr T's reaction to our budget. We walked towards Newbridge near Whitney, on the borders of the Cotswolds, soothed by the river air as we ambled along, watching the narrow boats, with their colourful painted decorations, drift past us. We were making for the Rose Revived pub and restaurant on the river bank in the heart of Oxfordshire as I was, by now, down in the dumps and in need of some comfort food.

Though not haute cuisine this pub serves meals that will keep anybody going in a crisis, like mixed grill that includes: Gloucestershire Old Spot pork sausage, with a Black Angus rump steak, chicken breast and gammon steak. In addition, they serve my favourite, sweet potato fries. All this at very reasonable prices.

As we got near the pub, thoughts of an early dinner made us move a little faster. To reach the pub we walked over a beautiful old bridge, one of the oldest crossing points on the river, which gave us a view of the Thames. This inn is a very popular stopping point for hikers on the towpath and the oldest part of the pub features an Inglenook fireplace perfect for roaring log fires in winter.

The Rose Revived's chief attraction is a terrace that overlooks the Thames and as it was still warm we sat at a table with a gorgeous view of the river. I told Randy that

Mr T's reaction was the reason I was down. The cloud that passed over his face could only mean one thing; the amount of money mentioned by us wasn't going to be enough. Suddenly, I was full of doubts. The Murgatroyds had sounded so negative. According to many friends and colleagues, buying a cottage had supposedly been an impossibility. That dream had come true, but now I wanted to extend the cottage. Was I pushing my luck trying to achieve the impossible again?

Two

WISTERIA COTTAGE
Minchinhampton, Uley, Nympsfield

"Ohh look there's an egg!" I was perched on a step ladder and almost tumbled off in my excitement. "And another one!"

The pair of doves, that had nested just above eye level in the honeysuckle vine in our garden, had produced two fragile-looking eggs and took turns sitting on them. I had taken a peek at them as we were having a relaxed breakfast nearby in our old wooden garden seat. This is my favourite breakfast spot, it had a high back and a small roof that provided shade, and though it was beginning to fall apart I couldn't bear to think of finding a replacement because it made such a romantic picture, its roof, in June, covered in masses of fragrant roses. I waited until both doves had flown away and then looked into the nest. Almost immediately there was a great squawking as Mama Dove had returned and dive bombed me. I climbed down the step ladder in a hurry. Randy laughed, at first I thought he was amused by my hasty retreat but it was an item in the morning newspaper that had caught his attention.

He read it as I finished my tea. "The British public's love of garden gnomes was in the spotlight this week when irate television viewers showered the Advertising Standards Authority with protests over an Ikea advertisement. This advert showed a garden gnome massacre, where an army of gnomes invaded the home of a family who were landscaping their garden. This family was then shown attacking the gnomes in more and more violent ways. Ikea's marketing manager was forced to confirm that, thanks to brave stunt doubles and clever post production editing, no gnomes were harmed in the making of the advertisement." I was happy to have English newspapers in my life again, which never fail to serve up Monty Python-style humour like this.

Randy read more bits out to me from the paper as I chuckled over them, sipped my tea and looked admiringly at our cottage. I still couldn't quite believe it was ours and I thought back to the first time I had actually stepped inside it.

That day we had turned off the main village street into a quiet side lane and, as we rounded a curve, there stood Wisteria Cottage in all its wonky glory just as it does now. It is seventeenth century with three floors, its uppermost level, which takes up the attic space, featured deep dormer windows with not one straight line anywhere in sight. Despite its three hundred-plus years of settling and warping, it has a great feeling of solidity, and glows from the sun's reflection off its honey-coloured Cotswold stone walls. The roof line dips crazily from the many years of supporting the original slate tiles. It is covered in lichen and untrimmed wisteria and roses ramble above the cottage's front door giving it just the right blowsy look.

There is no hallway and the front door opens directly into a very small living room typical of cottages of this era. The floor in here of uneven flagstones is original as is the Inglenook fireplace, with logs piled in two alcoves on either side.

Next to the living room is a small kitchen, also with a fireplace. Thankfully, the ceilings of the cottage are a comfortable couple of inches above my husband's head. Because this property has three floors, it is a cut above an ordinary worker's cottage and, consequently, constructed with slightly higher ceilings.

A charming circular stone staircase, which seems to have been hewn out of a wall next to the fireplace, leads upstairs to two very small bedrooms and a bathroom, all in good condition. Another circular staircase leads to the top floor and the main bedroom.

Up there, the exposed, crooked attic beams, their colour pale grey and chalky-looking with age, frame the room, creating the cosiest possible atmosphere. The dormer windows look out over a stunning view across the garden, tree tops and fields, dotted with sheep, beyond. Far in the distance, a river meanders through the landscape, its surface glittering in the sun.

When we first saw this room we stood in a daze for several moments, marvelling at how perfect it was before I noticed a door, somewhat above waist height, leading to another room. This, it turned out, led to the en-suite bathroom.

The previous owners were a lot shorter than us but even they had to crouch down a little to get through this door to the bathroom. The whole attic floor had been divided in two to create the main bedroom and bathroom. In order to have a properly sized door frame a beam would have to be moved but this had not been done – hence the Alice in Wonderland door. Once we entered the bathroom, however, we were stunned by the beauty of this room. Again the exposed beams, gnarled with age, gave it masses of character. An ancient, claw-foot bath was mounted on a dais in the centre of the room. This made it the perfect height for anyone bathing to catch the same spectacular view as that of the bedroom. I could tell it would be wonderful to have a long soak in this tub with nothing to do but drink a cocktail and take in the matchless Cotswold scenery.

A drawback with Wisteria Cottage was the tiny living room. However, I was relieved to find, when we were viewing it, that the Cotswold stone cart shed, at right angles to the cottage, could be converted into a good-sized living room as the space in between the two buildings could be joined up to the cottage.

As we had mentioned to the architectural planner, the last owners had obtained planning permission from the local council but had not carried out the work and passed their architect's plans on to us when they sold the house.

However, these lapsed plans would have to be redrawn. Permission had been obtained to join up the cottage with the cart shed to make a living room and for a small bathroom to be added into this space. We now wanted to amend the plans and add another small outbuilding more towards the back of the cottage into the join up. As we are such foodies it seemed appropriate that this outbuilding was thought to have once been a piggery. It would convert into a small study and office and would also be used as a recording studio for our vocal work. Upstairs we wanted to take the two very small bedrooms and make them into one decent sized guest bedroom and, of course, correct the height of the Alice in Wonderland door.

We were fortunate that nothing much needed doing outside. The garden with its well-stocked herbaceous borders, lily pond, Cotswold stone patio, garden seat covered in roses and that field view is not only wonderful but is in the right position to catch the sunset.

Once the renovation was finished we would have a new living room and the old postage stamp sized living room would become the dining room. In addition there would be a study in which to work, a reasonable sized guest bedroom and a small bathroom to double as a cloakroom on the ground floor.

I couldn't wait for it all to be completed so that we could spread out and start working and entertaining properly.

I had been reading up a lot more on all that was involved with building an extension and everything I saw indicated that when a listed building is involved the whole thing can, if things go wrong, turn into a money pit.

I started to get a cold, shivery feeling and realised that I needed to come up with more money quickly as this extension was already showing signs of being underfunded before we had even started.

A new money making scheme was what was needed but no new ones came to mind. I made a list of those I had going so far and then got on the computer and whizzed around my social media sites to see if anything new would get me fired up. Next, Randy and I discussed new ideas but he was as stumped as I was. I needed some inspiration but from where?

Eventually, my thoughts went back to my mother who, whenever she needed inspiration, would down huge quantities of tea to get her brainwaves juiced up. This was in addition to her usual big infusion of caffeine to get her up in the mornings.

My mother would sleep so soundly that surfacing from bed in the mornings was a major event. To wake up she relied on those machines that are a combination of alarm clock and automatic tea maker and had two of them parked by her bed. She would set one alarm to go off a few minutes after the other.

Before the first alarm sounded, an amazing series of clicks would herald the beginning of the whole tea-making process. Next, steam would rise and billow around the bedroom and, after some loud clanking noises, a few squeaks and the rattle of china a cascade of furiously boiling hot water would automatically pour over the tea leaves in the pot. Then an alarm that was louder than a fire engine would rouse Mum enough to grope for the pot and pour tea into a cup. She would chug down two or three cups, emptying the pot, then immediately conk out completely asleep again. After a few minutes the second alarm would go off and by the time she had finished the contents of that pot she would groggily surface, throw off the covers and stagger to the kitchen to put the kettle on for what she called 'a proper cup of tea'.

I decided to give some serious tea drinking a go, hard as it sounded on the body, as I was sure more money needed to be generated. I had some extra strong tea on hand, but once out of the package it looked a bit weak and wishy washy so I made a large pot and drank the lot. Before long I realised that I had under-estimated this tea's strength. My whole body was suddenly wired and I could feel the caffeine vibrating through me.

I closed my eyes and concentrated on my problem. How could I raise some more money? I meditated and the image of a screenplay I had recently written floated into my mind. This was an adaptation of my book *Cotswolds Memoir*. My goal was to get it produced as a movie. A big hill to climb for sure but I had done it once when the play I had created with my comedy troupe Bullshot Crummond had been produced as a movie under the title *Bullshot*, with Billy Connolly and Mel Smith.

Wow! Suddenly I had rockets going off in my brain. I saw a way to raise some money from my screenplay. First, I have to explain the lead up to my brainwave.

Several years ago, our neighbours who had become friends asked Randy and me to be godparents to their daughter. They were from China originally and so we became 'Gan Ma and Gan Ba' to their lovely girl. We had thoroughly enjoyed this assignment and followed through with attending school plays and many of the things godparents do. When I had invited these friends to a book signing of *Cotswolds Memoir* and mentioned that from it I was developing a movie script I was thrilled to find that Dad's new job was raising funds for movies and producing them. He liked my screenplay and agreed to take on the difficult process of getting it funded and produced. My screenplay was purchased and slotted into the production company's schedule and a date to begin shooting was fixed, as with most films, far into the future. Though the deal was done in Los Angeles it was determined that this movie would be shot in England with exterior scenes filmed in the Cotswolds. My script was now handed over to other writers for rewrites, as was common in Hollywood, and was out of my hands. I had put my script fee into the extension fund and it would go part way towards paying the building costs.

When my caffeine fix worked I realised I could make some money by renting out our cottage out as a film location to further fund the extension.

I got on the phone to Los Angeles and with my producer's help negotiated a fee with Chuck the location manager for the rental of the cottage for the movie shoot. He emailed me a contract and, although I would not receive the money until after the shoot was done, I could now borrow against it and have some hard cash to put towards the extension.

Film production moves very slowly and as the shoot wasn't scheduled for quite a while there would be plenty of time to get the extension done to be ready for the film crew. The amount I had raised from the location would definitely help and gave me the confidence that I would be able to come up with a few more money-making schemes like this. If these funds were put together with what Randy earned and with money coming in from reruns of our shows we could make it.

When Randy's family got in touch about their plans to come from America to visit England in December we had no qualms about inviting them to stay for the holiday season. The extension would be finished by then and the filming would not be scheduled until way afterwards. I was longing to host a country Christmas and it would be lovely to show off the renovated cottage and have the room to accommodate guests.

Feeling a whole lot better I turned to another one of my money making schemes, drumming up publicity to sell more books.

I had been invited to give an interview with Radio Gloucester for my book *Haunted Cotswolds* and suggested to the producers that the interview take place at Chevenage House which had been the subject of a chapter in this book. If this suggestion was taken up it would enable me to make another visit to this important historic building, combine it with the radio interview and, afterwards, more exploration of the Cotswolds.

Initially, when The History Press publishers had asked me to write *Haunted Cotswolds* I had turned their offer down. I confessed that I didn't believe ghosts existed. However, my editor insisted that this did not matter. She had read my book *Cotswolds Memoir* in manuscript and felt that my knowledge of the Cotswolds was what she was after. So I focused on writing about ghosts that haunted famous landmarks in the Cotswolds who were now so well-documented that they had become folklore. This enabled me to research and write about the history and architecture of this region and weave the information into these ghost stories.

I carefully planned our itinerary, arranging it to be a dazzling day out in the Cotswolds with all the attractions focused on one area so that not too much driving was involved.

As the attractions I had chosen were easily reached within relatively few miles of each other, visitors to the Cotswolds might find my itinerary for this day out a useful guide to a sample of the best of this fascinating area. All contact information and websites to the various activities are listed in the Visitor's Guide at the end of this narrative.

The following morning Randy and I set off early, first taking an idyllic, dawdling drive through the countryside as we headed for Tetbury, enjoying the views and spotting the photogenic black and white cows and a precious, new-born lamb tottering across the fields.

This whole area is so camera-ready, with glimpses of streams that feature stepping stones leading to perfect picnic spots and thousand-year-old wool churches, their spires soaring in the distance, that a spell of enchantment is cast by the sheer beauty of everything.

Chavenage House is considered the most perfect example of a Tudor mansion in the whole of Britain and is reputed to be haunted by several ghosts, the most notable of which is Charles I.

I recalled my experience of visiting this grand Tudor house for the first time when I carried out research for my book, and it was wonderful to have the opportunity to do so again.

Chevange has remained almost unchanged for five hundred years and there is a feeling in the air that Oliver Cromwell and his soldiers have been walking around its rooms only moments before. This mansion's bloodthirsty history speaks volumes and it is easy to imagine Civil War soldiers racing through its interior from dark nooks and crannies to stairwells and stables. Only two families have owned Chavenage House since Tudor times and the current owners, the Lowsley-Williams, have done a wonderful job of keeping it intact.

Nothing much has been altered since Edward Stephens, who became the owner of Chavenage in 1564, carried out most of the major renovations on the house.

I was particularly intrigued by the large stained glass windows that had been installed on the south side of the porch. Much of this glass is ecclesiastical, coming from the churches and monasteries in the area that were dismantled by Henry VIII during the Reformation. Apparently, Stephens used timbers from old galleons, broken up on the nearby River Severn. Some of these timbers bore carvings made by sailors to while away their time during long voyages. The reconstruction of the house, which was erected on the foundations of a building once owned by Princess Goda, sister of Edward the Confessor, was finished in 1576 and this date is carved into a pediment over the main door.

Edward Stephens passed Chavenage on to his son, Nathaniel, who occupied it during the time of the Civil War. Nathaniel, a leading parliamentarian, was a cousin of Oliver Cromwell.

Cromwell made a special visit to Chavenage House to persuade his cousin to authorise the execution of Charles I. King Charles was subsequently captured by Cromwell, tried, convicted of high treason and executed at the Palace of Whitehall. Although Stephens gave in to the intense pressure put upon him by Cromwell, at a later date he bitterly regretted this decision. Shortly afterwards, he was taken ill and met his death only four months after the execution of King Charles.

The bedroom in Chavenage House designated for Cromwell's visit is the magnificent Tapestry Room, now known as the Cromwell Room. I found it fascinating to enter this very same room with so much unchanged as if all these events had happened only yesterday.

I was interested to hear, too, of Chavenage's supernatural past. A number of the inhabitants of this house have, over the centuries, witnessed the same chilling event. They tell of seeing a spectral coach materialise on the forecourt of the mansion. Next, a ghostly, headless King Charles and the shade of Nathaniel Stephens climb into this coach and it speeds away, but before it reaches the gate of the manor it bursts into a huge ball of flame.

We arrived for my second visit to Chevenage to a very warm welcome by the entire Lowsley-Williams family. We were offered a coffee and before long were joined by the Radio Gloucester team. As it was a sunny day the interview was conducted in the grounds. It was very pleasant to be seated outside enjoying a lovely vista of the house, which is remarkably similar to an engraving that was made of it several hundred years ago. After I had been interviewed about my book, Mr Lowsley-Williams' son was asked what it had been like living in the house as a young lad. His reply amused everybody.

"My bedroom was haunted throughout my childhood. I was scared and would pull the covers over my head. It never occurred to me to complain to my parents because I thought every little boy's bedroom was full of ghosts."

My interview on Radio Gloucester seemed to go over very well. The first part was put out live and two more segments aired over the next couple of days.

Being able to roam all over Chavenage House with the Lowsley-Williams family pointing out all its treasures was an absolute joy. The interview was a lot of fun too and went off without a hitch, finishing early enough for us to do a bit more exploring before lunch.

As we motored on to our next stop I looked up the weather forecast in that day's newspaper, as the wind was picking up. It seemed appropriate that an item next to the forecast described the weather the day before in Scotland.

At the height of a gale, the Aberdeen harbour master radioed a coastguard on the spot and asked him to estimate the wind speed.

The coastguard replied, "I'm sorry but I don't have a gauge. However, if it is any help, the wind had just blown my Land Rover off the cliff."

By this time we had reached the small, unspoiled town of Minchinhampton, which is four miles south-east of Stroud in Gloucestershire.

I am particularly interested in market halls and this town features a perfectly preserved one from the 17th century, supported by sturdy stone columns. The church, set back from the high street, towers over the nearby cottages and dates from the 12th century, although it has been rebuilt several times. At some point this church lost the top half of its spire and the stump that is left is now crowned with a rather odd coronet contraption.

We ambled around, enjoying the fact that there were no tourists and that this sleepy town seemed little changed from three or four hundred years ago. The dozen or so shops are mostly clustered around the war memorial in the high street. We browsed in a few of these and then, to our delight, found a bit further along down a side street Taylor and Sons – a butcher's shop. Any town with a proper butcher gets top marks from me and straight away we bought an excellent free range chicken for the rotisserie on the barbeque. As we walked around we spotted ancient cottages with wonderfully wonky windows and Randy took lots of photos. We finished up buying a variety of cheeses from the delightfully named Woefuldane Café. This small but bustling organic dairy, we noted for another time, also serves tea, coffee and cakes.

This town was so charming we decided to try to come back for the Minchinhampton County Fayre which is held every second year.

Next, we set off for lunch and found the journey across Minchinhampton Common, which is administered by the National Trust, quite an adventure. Randy was forced to play cow-dodgems as cattle are allowed to wander freely across the common and have right of way. We came upon several of them lazily chewing the cud in the middle of the road and had to drive onto the roadside grass verge to go around them. Minchinhampton Common features ditches and mounds that form part of an Iron Age fort and is a Site of Special

Scientific Interest. There are important archaeological remains there, including The Bulwarks which are part of a defence system and also a noted long barrow, Whitfield's Tump. The common boasted one breathtaking view after another over the Severn Estuary across to Wales and to the east over the Golden Valley and on into the Cotswolds.

Tucked in beside the common on the Cirencester Road is The Ragged Cot, our destination for lunch, and it overlooks some of the finest views in the English countryside. It has been renovated with a fresh modern look that also retains many of its original features. This lovely inn offers delicious food and lunch or dinner can be taken inside its cosy rooms or on the outdoor patio. There is accommodation offered and this inn makes a good base from which to hike across Minchinhampton Common, and visit other historic towns in this part of the Cotswolds.

At The Ragged Cot we discovered that on occasion, 'pig's twigs' (pig's trotters) are on the menu and that dogs and Wellington boots are welcome. We were hungry after our busy morning so I had a starter of hand-picked crab with pink grapefruit and avocado salad and Randy had deep fried whitebait with garlic and parsley aioli.

I had brought the Saturday newspaper's magazine with me and as we waited for our next course I looked up the programming choices on television over the coming week. The often dire choice of programming in the summer in Britain seemed to have reached a new hilarious low. On offer was *Dogs on the Dole* – a look at the world of dog ownership in Britain's housing estates. *Hairy Biker's Food Tour of Britain, Nightmare Next Door Neighbours, Made in Britain*, where a former steeplejack visits a defunct pumping station in Sunderland, *Very British Problems* about the British population's excruciating inability to express emotions and *Don't Get Done in the Sun*, about holiday makers whose trips were ruined due to incorrect visas.

I had read these out to Randy and he was still laughing as our next course arrived. Tagliatelle with wild mushroom and sautéed spinach for me and Randy had settled on Barnsley lamb chop with roasted vine tomatoes. For desert we shared a dish of all-butter waffles with caramel sauce and ice cream. We were glad that our next activity, after a stroll around Uley village, was to be a strenuous hike to walk off the calories.

The village of Uley is about fifteen minutes by car from Minchinhampton. I like to find out what place names mean and Uley, which appears in the Domesday Book, is thought to translate to 'clearing in a yew wood'. How lovely if villages could still have names like that today. It would look so poetic on a letter head or on stationery.

Uley is between Dursley and Stroud in a deep, wooded valley on the Cotswold escarpment and features mostly eighteenth century houses. It is close to a Roman road and the Romans built a temple at West Hill near Uley on the site of a prehistoric shrine. During digging to lay a water pipe there in 1976 many finds were discovered. These included several writing tablets and a superb stone head of the Roman god Mercury, which is now in the British Museum. Our walk took us around past the Old Crown Pub, several antique stores and the village shop. We ended up at Uley's St. Giles's church which is Victorian and replaced earlier Norman and Saxon buildings. Next to the churchyard a path leads steeply up the hill to the Iron Age settlement of Uley Bury. Nearby is the Neolithic long barrow named Hetty Pegler's Tump after a previous landowner.

Our plan was to hike over this impressive fort dating from 300 B.C. It has far-reaching views over the Severn Vale and is situated on a spur of the Cotswold escarpment surrounded, except for the north corner, by steep natural slopes. There were once dwellings on the top of the fort but these have never been excavated. More than a mile in length the flat-topped fort was built by terracing a double line of ramparts into the hillsides. Uley Bury is well-known for its fossils of the lower Jurassic era.

It was the perfect, exhilarating hike, as the weather had now turned sunny and hot but with a breeze that was strong enough to blow all the cobwebs away. We were both puffing as we reached the top – a good hard climb – but so worth it for the absolutely spectacular views. The patchwork quilt of lovely fields stretched before us as far as the eye could see and the wind took our breath away. We couldn't tear ourselves away from the view and took picture after picture. We tried to imagine what it would have been like in 300 B.C. when the fort was built. It must have been unassailable by the enemy.

After we had circled around the top of the fort and climbed down we were hot and thirsty. We took a rest, sitting on a drystone wall that turned out to be outside the brewery for Uley Old Spot Ale, which is famous for producing this excellent beverage, one of my husband's favourites. A brewery worker saw us, stopped to chat, and offered us a very welcome complimentary glass of beer. Uley Brewery was established in the 1980s, in a Grade II listed building that is situated above a natural spring. This brewery uses Maris Otter barley malt, Fuggles (what a great name!) and Goldings hops, combined with a traditional method of fermentation. We took the ale gratefully as we were parched and it seemed like the best drink we had ever tasted, a great finish to our hike.

Refreshed, I realised we just had time to fit in my last item on the itinerary for the day, which was about a ten-minute drive away. On the way Randy challenged me to find yet another amusing item in this same day's newspaper and I won the bet we had easily.

When a homeowner rented out his furnished house he had imposed a strict 'no pets' ban. He made a spot check inspection of the house after noticing some damage in the garden.

Imagine his shock when he discovered a fully grown, fifty-stone black pig sprawled on the cream fitted carpet with its head resting on the leather sofa. The pig had been living in the house for some time and the damage was in the thousands of pounds. The pig, along with his owner the tenant, has now been evicted.

We arrived just in time for the main reason for coming this way, which was to visit Owlpen Manor, a gabled Tudor house, open to the public if groups are booked.

This manor house was rebuilt from Cotswold stone around the year 1450 but its origins date back to Saxon times. Its appearance is unbelievably romantic, quite surprisingly small and slightly ramshackle. It is framed by lovely trees in an isolated part of the countryside. It was originally occupied in 1174 by the Olepenne family, who were landowners and, in addition, benefactors to surrounding abbeys and hospitals. After many years of neglect it was repaired by Norman Jewson in 1925. Today it is the home of the Mander family.

By the beginning of the Tudor period, twelve generations of Olepennes had inhabited this manor. However, at this point the family's male line died out and the lands and manor were passed on to the Daunt family. This happened upon the marriage of Margery de Olepenne to John Daunt from nearby Wotton-under-Edge. The Daunt family occupied the manor until the male lineage of their family failed in 1803.

It is said that Queen Margaret of Anjou visited Owlpen Manor and slept in the great chamber, just before the Battle of Tewkesbury in 1471.

The terraced gardens were as impressive as the house and we had time for a quick tour before ordering the last tray of tea and scones with homemade strawberry jam, served at the tea room in the grounds before it closed.

Afterwards we ambled around the small village of nearby Nympsfield, which boasts a pub, The Rose and Crown, and lies six miles south-west of Stroud on the path of a Roman road just east of the Cotswold Edge in Gloucestershire.

My husband took some great photos of the gargoyles and grotesques on the 19th century church which has an interesting clock and a set of turret stairs.

I later discovered that Nympsfield is a blend of Celtic and Old English and means 'Open land by the holy place'.

Nympsfield appears in the Domesday Book. However, there is even earlier recorded history of it as it can traced back to 862 A.D.

The Neolithic Nympsfield Long Barrow is nearby and also close is the spooky manor house, Woodchester Mansion, an unfinished gothic curiosity, which is open to the public. This manor is said to be full of supernatural spirits which I write about in detail in my book *Haunted Cotswolds*.

We set off for home, tired but happy. It certainly had been a dazzling day out, and we had packed in everything on the itinerary.

We arrived home to find a letter from our architectural planner setting a date for him to come to our cottage to look at what was needed and discuss our plans for an extension. I couldn't wait to get started but my excitement was tinged with a feeling of apprehension as I had never attempted anything like this before.

Three

DOWNTON ABBEY DISCOVERED
Bampton, Little Rissington, Minster Lovell

"Thought you might like a game of croquet – so we're loaning you an extra set we have."

"How lovely, thanks so much."

"Yes, but don't play croquet with my wife. She'll knock your ball into the stinging nettles," said Brigadier Murgatroyd as he set up the metal hoops on some flat lawn by our apple tree.

We made a pot of tea and served a delicious cream and strawberry roulade that I had just finished decorating.

We sat in the garden and discussed the architectural planner's visit that was coming up soon.

I confessed to my nervousness about our upcoming renovation.

"You can fix these listed cottages but the planning committee will only give you the proper permission if the building materials used are 'like for like'. Do you understand?" said Mrs Murgatroyd.

"No," I replied.

"Well, if your roof has Stonesfield slate tiles and it needs rebuilding then that is what has to replace them. Finding and buying these original materials like this can become ruinously expensive you know."

Mrs Murgatroyd didn't notice that I had turned pale, as this was news to me.

"How's your roof?" she demanded.

Without waiting for an answer she continued. "Lots of people around here have a 'roof fund'. Replacing the entire roof takes every penny and keeps them poor for the rest of their lives. They have to organise fund raisers as there is no hope of saving up enough otherwise.

"Don't forget that signs have to be posted on your gate and in the newspaper to inform your neighbours of what you intend to do. And the conservation officer doesn't like reflections, you know?"

"Reflections? What do you mean?"

"Double glazing, of course. Doesn't give the same reflection as single panes, so you can't have that."

As Mrs Murgatroyd continued on I thought about the possibility of just scrapping the whole idea of an extension and trying to make do with Wisteria Cottage with no alterations. But I realised if we were ever to be comfortable and for me to have a place to write, a work space and a bigger living room was an absolute necessity. On some occasions this work space would have to do double duty as a sound-proofed recording studio for our vocal work. I tried to quell my anxiety as Mrs Murgatroyd chatted on about the perils of altering period cottages.

I gave a sigh of relief when eventually her conversation zoomed off in a completely different direction, as it quite frequently did. Somehow, Mrs M got on to talking about her son and how adventurous he had been as a teenager.

"My boy was always getting into scrapes and in those days he was absolutely besotted with hang gliding. He had to be high up on the side of a hill to catch the wind, in order to take off, you see. He needed someone to hold on to his legs and weigh him down until he said the word. He took me with him up to a very big hill and made this my task. When he shouted 'Now, Mama' I would let go and off he would sail.

"On one occasion I was holding on to his legs as usual but before he could tell me to let go a massive gust of wind swept him off the hill and took me with him. My son had the hang glider but I was merely holding on to his legs. As I felt my hands slipping I could just see the headlines: 'Daughter of baron hang glides off a mountain with disastrous results.' But we sailed over a spur of rock that jutted out and when the wind dropped for a few seconds, my son shook me off his legs and I landed on some shrubs so, except for a couple of bruises, no harm done."

We couldn't get enough of these wonderfully goofy stories from the Murgatroyds and after several more were recounted we ended the afternoon's visit with a game of croquet where Mrs M did indeed knock my ball into the stinging nettles, beating me and everybody else.

After the Murgatroyds had departed I discussed our situation with Randy. What they had said about roof funds and 'like for like' replacements of original materials had really scared me. My recent money making scheme, which had produced a loan against the location contract for the movie, might be a drop in the ocean instead of a sizeable contribution to the budget.

Our funds had been low to begin with, as producing the down payment for Wisteria Cottage had taken most of what we had. When we applied for a loan for the cottage we asked for more than the purchase price but did not get as much as we wanted. We had been so caught up in the romantic notion of buying a cottage, against all odds, that we had not had the time or energy to give a lot of thought to how we were going to finance this extension.

Also, it was becoming clear that getting planning consent from the local council could possibly be more complicated than we thought.

We had bought Wisteria Cottage on an adjustable mortgage, meaning our payments would change depending on whether the interest rate went up or down. At this point in time the interest rate was low, but we knew we couldn't depend on that always being the case. That meant that our expenses could possibly go up even further.

Because we had bought the cottage on 'a wing and a prayer' we needed to get building work done fairly speedily. This would enable us to rent out Wisteria Cottage in the winter months when we were back working in Hollywood.

The extra income from the rental of the cottage would mean that we could make the mortgage payments and remain solvent. Now we were getting the uncomfortable feeling that there could be a chance of running out of money before the building work on the extension could be completed.

There was the possibility of my husband helping with some of the building work. He is very good at this kind of thing, having worked as a builder when he was a student but he needed to be working too to finance all the outgoings and so did I. It was unclear at this point how much his 'sweat equity' could lay off some of the building costs.

Having heard from the Murgatroyds about using only original materials we now realised that estimates for the building work were definitely going to be higher than anticipated.

Nothing could be done until estimates came in but Randy suggested that we might feel better if we took a look at a reclamation yard to see if the building materials of the right period could be purchased to save on costs.

He pointed out that the positive side of building this extension meant that we would need to roam all over the Cotswolds shopping at reclamation yards, car boot sales and antique shops and this would enable me, at the same time, to do the thing I loved best, explore the Cotswolds.

I immediately planned an itinerary around the visit to a reclamation yard and we set off early the next morning.

First, we stopped for breakfast in the beautiful medieval town of Burford, which I describe in my last book, at The Priory Café on the high street. This little café, although serving simple fare, is the perfect place for a good old-fashioned English breakfast and much else besides.

Sometimes we would sit inside at our favourite table in the window, where the view of the high street makes for excellent people watching. But on a sunny day, a table in the quiet and pretty patio garden at the back of the café is hard to beat.

We ordered our usual: a full house breakfast of eggs, bacon, sausage, grilled mushrooms and tomatoes with toast and marmalade.

As we waited for our meal, I admired the lovely array of flowers growing in the Priory Café's garden while Randy read me a snippet from the morning's newspaper.

He laughed as he quoted: "A North West Gas spokesman commented on a complaint from a customer about a large gas bill. We agree it was rather a large bill for the time of year," he said. "It is possible that the customer has been charged for the gas used up during the explosion that destroyed his house." Several people at the next table overheard this and chortled, muttering 'Typical'.

Although it is hard to get up from the table after a full English breakfast at the Priory Café I knew it would give us the necessary carbohydrate loading for all that we had planned for the busy morning.

Before we reached the reclamation yard I suggested our next stop should be Bampton. I was happy to find that by visiting this unspoiled village I could combine Cotswold exploring with taking a peek at the locations used for filming *Downton Abbey*. Not only is it interesting to see where these scenes were shot but there are many other attractions in Bampton that would make a leisurely sojourn there memorable.

Bampton, or as it was once known Bampton-in-the-Bush, is in the county of Oxfordshire in the Thames Valley and is about four and a half miles south-west of Witney.

A star was born when *Downton Abbey*'s creator Julian Fellowes stayed with friends in beautiful 'forgotten-by-time' Bampton and 'discovered' this lovely village just as Hollywood discovered Lana Turner in Schwab's drugstore in 1937.

Bampton was chosen to co-star as Downton Village with leading lady Highclere Castle playing the fictitious home of the Granthams, supposedly situated somewhere between Ripon and Thirsk. But, in a familiar Hollywood story, rising star, the Cotswolds, may have stolen the film clear away from the name above the title.

It could happen again shortly as the Cotswolds again gets 'ready for its close up Mr deMille' in *Downton Abbey* – the movie which is already in the pipeline.

The television locations for *Downton Abbey*'s filming are so popular with viewers that they have become characters in their own right. Fans swarm to visit from every corner of the globe and tour buses appear wherever filming for Downton has taken place.

Box office is the bottom line in the business of show and *Downton Abbey*'s figures are eye-poppingly astonishing. A mere ten million viewers watch the series in Britain, dwarfed by twenty-six million in America and those numbers are left in the dust with a whopping one hundred and sixty million viewers in China.

Bampton may be the co-lead of Downton but there are also some fine cameo appearances by Cogges Farm, Swinbrook, Shilton and on the outer edge of the Cotswolds, The Great Coxwell Barn. More on those cameo appearance in a later chapter.

In fact, the Cotswolds has been waiting in the wings for the last five or six hundred years for its fifteen minutes of fame, maturing like a fine claret and looking so good it doesn't need even a miniscule amount of make-up. The Cotswolds is so camera-ready that it truly is, as Humphrey Bogarde growls in *The Maltese Falcon*, 'the stuff that dreams are made of'.

We immediately spotted Bampton's church, renamed St. Michael and All Angels in *Downton Abbey* and the background for countless Sunday morning gatherings and weddings in the series.

It is actually called the church of St. Mary of the Virgin, dates from the 12th century and, like many ancient buildings in Britain, was built on the foundations of an earlier structure, incorporating parts of the older building in the new edifice. St. Mary's was erected on the site of an Anglo-Saxon minster. The tower was the only feature of the minster that was spared and it is now part of the rebuilt church. St. Mary's is also distinguished by its magnificent 13th century spire. William the Conqueror gave this church to the Bishop of Exeter and it has been altered and added to many times through the centuries.

Our visit had coincided with a day that filming was scheduled and, being fans of *Downton Abbey*, we were excited to see that the village was dressed for scenes to be shot. Church View is home to two fictional pubs and is the site of the Downton Fair. One of the cottages in Church View had been cleverly turned into The Dog and Duck pub and another The Grantham Arms. A war memorial had been added in front of the church by the film crew and other set pieces transformed Bampton into Downton village.

Film extras were waiting to walk by in a scene that was about to be shot and cameras and crew were grouped around the church. In the distance we even glimpsed the actor Hugh Bonneville, who plays Lord Grantham in the series. We couldn't believe our luck and stopped to watch a couple of scenes being filmed.

When a break was called in the filming we strolled on a few yards and recognised 'Downton Hospital', which appears in the second season of the series. According to Pevsner and Sherwood's book, *The Buildings of England*, this building was once the old Grammar School of St. Mary's Church, built in 1653. It is now used as the Bampton Community Archive and displays exhibitions and a selection of *Downton Abbey* memorabilia.

Within a few yards, in the opposite direction, we found the Old Rectory, now named Churchgate House, which is close by St. Mary's Church. This was used for exterior shots of Isobel Crawley's house in *Downton Abbey*. Only a little of this building is visible from behind a high wall but is still quite recognisable from the scenes in the series.

The south side of this building is late 17th century and features five bays. The back of the house is older, with a 16th century arched stone doorway and in the garden wall there is a stone inscribed with the date 1546. Next to the Rectory are 17th century stables with a gabled dovecote built over them. The interior scenes of Isobel Crawley's house, however, were filmed at Hall Place near Beaconsfield in Buckinghamshire.

It was fascinating to stroll around this village and remember where various scenes in *Downton Abbey* had taken place.

When I chatted with some of the locals I discovered that Bampton has some wonderfully eccentric annual customs, celebrated every year, which could be combined with viewing the Downton locations when fans of the show and visitors make their way to this interesting village.

Once a year, on the Saturday of the Spring Bank Holiday, there is a bizarre pub crawl organised by the Society for the Preservation of Ancient Junketing, known as The Bampton Shirt Race. In past times the runners in this race were dressed in night-gowns and would compete in pairs with one runner pushing the other in a trolley (don't ask why).

There was a time when there were fourteen pubs in Bampton and the race stops at every location for the competitors to down a large quaff of beer. Many of those public houses have now been converted to private residences but a stop at these former pubs is still included in the race. Nowadays, the race consists of larger teams using many different kinds of cobbled-together vehicles, such as prams, wheelbarrows and even wheelie bins. These are used to transport the competitors who are costumed in outlandish fancy dress. There are prizes for the best outfits.

Bampton is also well-known for its Morris dancing which has been practised in the village since the late eighteenth century. The town supports three world-renowned Morris dance teams and the dancing is performed throughout the Monday of the Spring Bank Holiday in the latter part of May, beginning at 8.30am.

I adore Morris dancing even though I think it is an extraordinary thing for grown men to do. The Morris dancers' costumes are a hoot, they could be Tyrolean mountain climbers from *The Sound of Music*, with Christmas bells tied around their knees. When they dance there is an explosion of leaping up and down, accompanied by much manic slapping of knees and ankles, like demented boy scouts who have just been stung by a swarm of bees.

Another charming tradition in Bampton is May garland making by children. This event originated several centuries ago and takes place at 11am in the market square on the Monday of the Spring Bank Holiday.

A not-to-be missed Donkey Derby is run on the Monday of the August Bank Holiday, also organised by the Society for the Preservation of Ancient Junketing. This begins at 2pm at Sandford's Field. In addition to the donkey races, where all the jockeys are children, there are bric-a-brac stalls, skittles, Aunt Sally, crockery smashing and much more.

If all this isn't enough we were very interested to find (being actors ourselves) that a band of Mummers perform plays on Christmas Eve every year. These plays have been performed since the nineteenth century in Bampton but are most likely much older. The Mummers' dramas have been handed down through family tradition by word of mouth as no scripts exist.

After this whirlwind of activities a little refreshment might be in order. Bampton's pubs include: The Morris Clown Pub in the High Street, The Romany Inn on Bridge Street and The Horse Shoe on the High Street.

Just five minutes car ride from Bampton in Buckland Marsh is The Trout at Tadpole Bridge. It is on the banks of the Thames and well-known for its fine dining.

Bampton might look like a sleepy little village on Downton but it seems the local residents and the visitors who join in are having more fun than anybody knew.

Finally, we headed for Cotswolds Reclamation Yard. This was a bit of drive from Bampton so I read Randy an item from the newspaper that I had brought with me as we motored along.

Apparently, during a science fiction convention in Norwich a man dressed as a *Dr Who* character was assaulted by another fellow in a Darth Vader costume and when police were called he wanted to press charges.

Police decided that assembling an identity parade from over three hundred people dressed in Darth Vader costumes would not be practical.

This had followed another incident when two men dressed as Ozzy Osbourne and Elvis Presley attacked an off-duty policeman who happened to be dressed in a

Wyatt Earp costume (it is not clear why). Does anyone in Norwich dress normally?

There is nothing like an English newspaper to put a smile on my face.

I already had one actually, as the gorgeous Cotswold scenery was looking particularly beautiful. It was a sunny day and we took the little country lanes instead of the more direct main road route. Driving slowly along with the windows down, stopping now and then to photograph tucked-away ancient cottages and centuries-old barns was a joy. Wildlife, including pheasants, hares and muntjacs often skittered across in front of us. Occasionally, a farmer would guide his sheep or cattle across the lane to another field. It's great to see the cows, sheep and green fields up close with the occasional highlight of a few fields of bright yellow blossom, glowing lavender or crimson poppies, depending on the season. Sometimes we would come across a perfect, off-the-beaten-track small village or hamlet looking exactly the same as it had for the last six hundred years. It is possible to drive on these small lanes for miles without encountering another car and the feeling of getting away from the madding crowds into the peace of this glorious countryside with its gently rolling hills is my idea of heaven.

We were so enjoying the lovely day that we decided on the spur of the moment to take another detour on our way to the reclamation yard to explore Little Rissington on the eastern slopes of the Windrush Valley. It was good to stretch our legs as we strolled around this small village, which has pleasing views over the nature reserve of nearby Bourton-on-the-Water.

St. Peter's Church is not visible from the village so a local directed us to a path across a field where it stands isolated in the middle of a meadow. Apparently, at one time there were buildings all around this church but at some point this part of the village was dismantled. It took a five-minute hike to reach the church which is on a promontory and commands spectacular views across the Windrush Valley. In local custom, traditionally, a bride must be lifted over the church gate by her groom, although it has been known that assistance has sometimes been provided by the best man!

This church has an interesting south doorway which is Norman. Inside, we were immediately stuck by the arcade of two 12ᵗʰ century Romanesque arches which divide the nave from the north aisle. These are an impressive five-feet eight-inches in circumference. However, it was disappointing to see that the remainder of the interior of the church had been destroyed in a dreadful Victorian refit.

We spent a while looking at a stained glass window in the church, simple and elegant in design, dedicated to the men who were stationed at the R.A.F. in Little Rissington from 1938 to 1976. It is a poignant reminder that the war had such an impact even in this peaceful corner of the world.

Next, we drove a couple of miles over to Upper Rissington where Cotswold Reclamation is situated.

This treasure trove of wonders sells reclaimed and antique building materials. It is situated on the A424 between Burford and Stow-on-the Wold in the village of Upper Rissington. See contact details at the end of this narrative.

For some reason I had imagined that a yard like this would consist of huge piles of junk and to find anything would mean scrambling over mountains of cast-off, recycled detritus. But in this yard everything was laid out in a very orderly way. In fact, there were so many interesting items to see and I got so absorbed in studying numerous antique pieces that I quite forgot that we were supposed to be getting an idea of what would be appropriate for our extension. In addition to the outside yard there was an antique shop off to the side filled with vintage mirrors, pine dressers, glass ware and carved stone fireplaces.

Outside, the stone and statuary section was a revelation. There were elegant old balustrades, a feathered griffin, an ancient farm water trough and a weathered, stone cauldron that looked as if it belonged to the three witches of *Macbeth*. There was even an antique stone quern, used for grinding flour.

Most interesting of all though were three stone-carved heads that looked 14th century to me. They appeared to have been taken from a dismantled church or perhaps a vicarage. One carving was of a woman wearing a wimple, another was a stern-looking warrior and the last a prince or a king. They were beyond our budget but would look wonderful worked into the wall of our extension or in a dry stone wall in the garden.

We thoroughly enjoyed browsing through lovely old roof tiles, wrought iron gates, worn Cotswold flag stones, reclaimed oak beams and much more.

On their web site there is an invitation by the owners of the reclamation yard to haggle, which I thought was very civilized of them. Randy was happy as he could see that materials from this yard could help enormously to defray the building material costs on the extension. He was particularly interested in the flag stones to fill where the new floor would be needed to join up the cottage with the outbuildings. I thoroughly enjoyed visiting this reclamation yard as it was almost like an architectural museum filled with fascinating historic artefacts. It makes for a unique stopping off point for visitors interested in the history of the Cotswolds.

Next, we drove, again through the back lanes, to Minster Lovell. I had long wanted to explore this ancient ruin, which is two and a half miles west of Witney in Oxfordshire and can be reached from the A40 and then the B4047. I had found a four-mile circular walk that would begin and end there but first we made for the banks of the Thames a few yards from the ruin, which is an ideal picnic spot. I spread out our light picnic lunch on a table cloth on the grass. There were willow trees on the banks for shade, which was fortunate as now the day had heated up considerably.

Tapenade is delicious in a sandwich and I had made a big batch of a pesto version of this spread. Mine contained walnuts, the pulp of roasted garlic, fresh basil and olive oil all mashed together in a food processor. This mixture takes well to freezing so I had made lots of it and stored it divided into numerous small glass containers. Randy spread this Pesto Tapenade onto some delicious spelt bread we had bought in Huffkins of Burford that morning. He then added thin slices of turkey, some butter lettuce and a little pickled ginger. Next, a couple of small heirloom tomatoes were added to the sandwich platter for garnish. This made a tasty light lunch and with it we shared a half bottle of crisp sauvignon blanc, which we knew would help to fortify us on our upcoming hike. Afterwards, we relaxed on the riverbank and Randy laughed as I read him yet another amusing snippet from my newspaper which seemed to have a surfeit of them on this particular day.

Police arrested a masked man who held up a grocery store in Clitheroe, Lancashire and demanded cash from the till. The robber was shocked to find that the worker behind the till was his mother-in-law. He changed his voice to stop her recognising him but she was not fooled and turned him in to the police. She said, "He was shouting and swearing but I knew who he was right away. He has a peculiar walk and although he had his hood pulled down and a mask on his face I recognised him a mile off."

The sun was hot enough to make us both very sleepy so we took a 15-minute nap before having some coffee from a Thermos I had brought with us and packing up our picnic.

Next we strolled along nearby Minster Lovell High Street, which features picture-perfect thatched, stone cottages, then crossed farmland and followed an ancient lane to reach the nearby village of Crawley. This circular hike can be gleaned from an Ordinance Survey map. I had previously bought these maps to cover the entire Cotswolds and they proved very useful in planning hikes. See my choice of maps at the end of this narrative.

This hike features a good variety of woodland, hills to climb, kissing gates and riverside meadows. On our return the hike took us alongside the River Windrush and back to Minster Lovell.

We marvelled at the dramatic sight of the fragments of Minster Lovell Hall, with its impressively massive walls silhouetted against the sky and framed by green fields and the river.

We roamed around the ruins, which are maintained by English Heritage, and dates from the first half of the 15th century. It was built by William, the 7th Baron of Tichmarsh. The walls that are still left standing loom over the great room, which measures 50 by 26 feet. Minster Lovell was built on the foundations of an earlier 12th century manor and the hall has been a ruin since it was dismantled in 1747. It was originally a fortified manor house built in the form of a quadrangle with one end open to the River Windrush. We took lots of photographs and climbed an open staircase, giving us more of an overview of the ruins, the dovecote and the surrounding farm land.

We spent the best part of the afternoon exploring the ruins as there was so much to see. First, the hall itself and next the medieval dovecote, which has been carefully restored, and finally St. Kenelm's a fine 15th century cruciform church with distinctive vaulting. It contains the tomb of a knight – thought to be that of William Lovell.

Next we walked through the churchyard and over several fields until we reached the Old Swan Inn and Minster Mill, our destination for an early dinner. The Old Swan nestles in an idyllic setting of 60 acres of woodland, orchards and a mill stream and has recently been treated to a tasteful renovation, which retained all its original architectural features.

This 15th century building could not look more romantic with its lichen-covered slate roof and slightly askew half-timbers, which are somewhat hidden by the rambling vines that cover a good part of the building. There are a number of hotel rooms tucked up in the eaves and very cosy they must be too. Apparently, when Maggie Smith was working on *Downton Abbey*, she would stay here, though the rest of the cast stayed elsewhere, and I can quite see why.

We wandered over to the Victorian mill next door which now houses the newer hotel rooms and could not believe how beautiful it all was. Accommodation was shown to us as some friends visiting from America wanted to book a hotel. A member of the friendly staff took us to a room, which was furnished with luxurious fabrics and featured a scenic garden view. Weeping willows bordered the calm waters that flowed by this riverside setting and we could see why Visit Britain has awarded this hotel its top five stars.

Outside the inn, elegant wrought-iron tables and seating were arranged by the river, a perfectly lovely place to sit and watch the swans and ducks drift by.

We wandered back next door to the Old Swan and took a look at the inviting bar, which in winter features log fires. Several guests were lounging in comfortable armchairs, drinking complimentary sloe gin. The dining room features its original, very impressive, exposed beams and we took our drink out on the outside terrace which overlooks a pretty garden.

For dinner my husband chose venison which had been hung for 28 days, while I was very happy with a lighter meal of two starters – potted shrimp and a delicious coarse pâté.

When we got home Randy looked over the notes he had made at the reclamation yard and did some research to see how much we could save with the building materials that were available there.

It had been a good day, lots of exploring in the halcyon Cotswolds and a small step forward on the extension. In the meantime, I tried to convince myself that there was no point in getting anxious until the estimate for the building work actually came in.

Four

RUSTY THE IRON AGE MAN
Chipping Campden, Bourton on the Hill, Ebrington

"I think you should have a window here," said Mr T, our architectural planner. "That would bring extra light into this area." He pointed to a sketch he was making of the section that would join our cottage to the cart shed which was to be the new living room.

"Yes," I said, "that would be great, I would like as much light as possible."

"Fine, a window it is," he said breezily. He quickly sketched the connecting section that joined up the cart shed and the piggery and then added it into a program in his laptop of a three-dimensional realisation of the extension.

It was thrilling to see the interior of the new extension come to life and he seemed to have the whole thing handled quite nicely.

Shortly after that Mr T got back to us with an estimate of building costs to complete the extension.

"Are your fingers crossed?" asked Randy.

I gripped his hand tightly as we waited for Mr T's pronouncement.

Of course, it was more than we had anticipated. We both groaned.

"Can it be brought down if I do some of the work?" asked Randy

"Most likely, and I will try and shave off as much as I can, too," he replied.

Looking at me, Randy said, "If we borrow a bit more to cover the higher cost of the estimate and then the wait for the planning permission is not too long – we can just do it, I think."

Plans were drawn up. Mr T sent what seemed like mountains of paperwork to be filled in. These went back and forth and left my head spinning.

In the meantime, we started on the renovations that we could do ourselves. We knew we could save costs on stripping the beams in the cart shed that would eventually be our new living-room. These had been painted over a number of times through the centuries and were now a sooty black. The beams would look so much better stripped down to the bare wood.

Stripping wood can be a long process and I had asked advice about it from some of my friends. Several of them offered to come over and help and at first I declined but my kind pals refused to listen and made a date to come over. Four couples turned up a few nights later, wearing old clothes and bringing safety goggles and gloves.

I had been advised to use Peel Away. This product is amazing. It is designed to remove up to 32 layers of paint in one application. But there are several steps to doing this and it is quite time consuming. Peel Away was designed to make it safe to remove layers of old lead-based paints without the use of a heat gun or a sanding machine, as these methods can pollute the environment.

I knew I was on to the right thing when the description of this product stated that it is approved by The National Trust, English Heritage and The Building Conservation Trust. It has been used for a number of high profile restoration projects, including interiors at The British Museum and intricate panelling at the Victoria and Albert Museum.

A friend had put me on to Peel Away when she viewed an episode of *Restoration Home*, where a beautiful Georgian mansion was restored to its former glory. In this programme, over 200 years of paint is removed from complex mouldings to spectacular effect. Close ups of painted plasterwork before this treatment show it to be so over-painted that it resembled an out of focus photograph. After the Peel Away poultice and blankets have been applied, allowed to do their magic and then pulled away, the intricate sculpture of the plasterwork was revealed to be startlingly sharp-edged and 'in focus'.

The paint-stripping party was a lot of fun and as my friends worked on the beams our chatter evolved into a competition to see who had experienced the most disastrous do-it-yourself or building catastrophe.

My friend Howard made a good start when he talked about the time he borrowed a friend's brand new luxury four by four van, for a trip to the recycling centre, with strict instructions to return it in perfect condition. The next day as he was driving he was forced to break hard to avoid a driver running a red light. He avoided a collision but the 20 tins of old paint he had in the back of the vehicle hurtled forward and smashed into the back seat. Their poorly secured lids flew off with the impact and five gallons of multi-coloured paint sloshed over the seats, soaking Howard and the entire interior of the van. It cost him all his savings to get the interior cleaned out, by which time the radio no longer worked.

As we laughed at the horror of this scenario Randy remembered the story of a student at his college who promised to look after his parent's house when they departed for a holiday.

The student had just a few friends over for a quiet barbeque one evening and during this one of the guests wanted to show off her newly-acquired cheerleading skills. She juggled cheerleader batons with flaming tips – throwing them high in the air to the admiration of the guests. However, when she dropped one, the family dog seized the still flaming baton and scrambled under the narrow crawl space of the house with it gripped between his jaws. After a few moments the dog ran back out but he no longer had the baton, and it was unreachable in the crawl space. Before the fire department arrived a good portion of the house had burned down.

Another friend, James, talked about being asked to house sit a flat for a friend.

This flat had taken two years to renovate and was furnished with impeccable taste. James, overjoyed with this offer, promised to take great care of everything. All went well and on the last night of his stay he threw a small dinner party. As he served the meal James put a hot dish on a white granite dining table. This table turned out not to be granite but antique milk glass. Suddenly, with a loud crack, the end of the table fell off, taking the hot dish of food with it and shattered in pieces, damaging the floor. As James frantically searched the Internet for ways to fix everything, one of the guests rather too exuberantly flopped onto a fancy hammock hanging by a window. It turned a complete circle taking him with it. His legs were flung out and one foot went through a window pane and the other smashed a rare, antique Sanskrit-engraved vase. Another guest was so startled by the smashing glass that she spilled red wine on a one-of-a-kind 18th century, toile sofa cushion. By now James was becoming unhinged as he ran from one disaster to the next. He put the sofa cushion in a washbasin full of water in the bathroom but before he could get the stain out he was called away by one of the guests who had noticed that the red wine had also stained the cream, crushed velvet sofa. James tried rubbing salt in the stain and blotting it with paper towel. Shortly, a frantic banging summoned James to the front door of the flat where he found a man shouting at him in another language and holding up a large, ruined painting. The cushion that James had been washing in the bathroom had blocked the overflow and as the tap had been left running this man's studio was flooded on the floor below, ruining his water colour paintings. These had been commissioned by a celebrity client and were to be unveiled the next evening for the house warming party of his new manor house which was to be attended by Royalty. James was mortified that he had turned into a one-man wrecking crew.

By now the Peel Away poultice had been applied and Randy served one of his signature Le Crueset dishes.

This cast iron cooking pot makes everything taste absolutely delicious and works like a sort of mini AGA. He brought it in, lifted the lid and the scent of the braised Cotswolds lamb wafted around the room, causing the appropriate approving comments from our guests. After searing lamb chops Randy had baked them slowly with a slew of small organic onions and mushrooms and a splash of red wine. When the lamb was cooked, Randy had deglazed the bottom of the Le Crueset on the stove-top with some Madeira wine. This dish was served on a nutty brown and wild rice mix. I filled some tumblers with wine, threw a few old cushions around and we sat cross-legged on the floor of the cart shed and dug in.

After dinner, our guest Susan told another DIY-related story about the rewiring of her house.

"This was a long job so Bob and I left the electrician to get on with it and we took off to do some errands, telling him we'd be back in about three hours. But after about 20 minutes I realised that I had forgotten some paperwork we needed so we came back to collect it. When we came in we found the electrician standing there stark naked except that he was wearing a set of my sexiest, skimpy underwear."

The laughter that greeted this story made it the clear winner of the evening and everybody was still chuckling about it as they departed.

After everybody had left, Randy and I discussed what our friend James, who owned a listed cottage, had said as he chatted during dinner. He told us that the planning permission for his renovation had taken longer to come through because his home was thought to be situated on top of an archaeological site. Apparently, the planning authorities know the location of almost every major archaeological site in the country. If building work on a listed property is scheduled on or near one of these sites, or for example, near a Roman road, this triggers a visit by a planning officer who specialises in archaeology. If it is warranted, the council will carry out an excavation to see if there are any archaeological earthworks or finds.

After this the planning authority will determine what action to take.

If archaeology is found then a number of different solutions may be applied. It could mean that the building is moved to another part of the site or a part of it is redesigned in order not to disturb the earthworks.

Sometimes, in order to determine if there are archaeological finds on the site, a trench would be dug to see if there is anything of importance.

I am fascinated by archaeology digs and, initially, I thought it would be thrilling to find some precious artefacts on our land. However, I discovered that if this happened it could mean risking financial ruin, which could come about if the land had to be excavated to uncover say an Iron Age settlement that could result in building work being held up for months.

Something of this nature happened to one of our favourite pubs, the Horse and Groom in Bourton-on-the-Hill, as we were to discover when we visited it before a radio interview I had scheduled nearby.

This pub is in the more northerly part of the Cotswolds so it seemed a good opportunity to make a day of it and choose a hike up there as well. We used the Horse and Groom as our starting point to plan a three-mile circular walk, from the footpaths shown on our Ordinance Survey maps, that would lead us back to the this pub in time for lunch.

It was a warm, sunny day and we climbed higher and higher in the car towards Bourton-on-the-Hill taking in the gorgeous views that I knew would be featured in our walk. We parked at the Horse and Groom, having booked our lunch a few days before, and asked permission to leave the car there for our hike. I packed plenty of water and a compass in our backpacks.

At the pub we seemed to be at the highest point of Bourton-on-the-Hill and spent a few minutes enjoying the spectacular vistas of rolling hills for miles around and gazing at the quaint little town spread out below us. We took a south-west direction from the Horse and Groom and strolled downhill about 50 or so yards before stopping to explore the church. Dedicated to St. Lawrence, this church is perched in a wonderfully lofty location overlooking Moreton-in-the-Marsh and the whole Evenlode Valley. We were stunned by the views and imagined parishioners all through the centuries having to tear themselves away from this gorgeous scenery to go in to the church for the service. I had read up on the architecture of this building and found that although little of the original church remains there are still some stone pillars that date from the year 1157 on the south side of the nave. These simple and elegant pillars were much bigger and sturdier than I had imagined, which was perhaps why they had been incorporated into the subsequent building stages of the church and are still here to this day. There had been extensive rebuilds of this church in the 14th and 15th centuries when a new chancel, the east window, the north nave and tower were added. There were lots of fascinating details to see, including a fine series of five grotesques and dragons carved on the south door.

The 15th century stone screen has an interesting history. It was not part of the original church but was rescued from a builder's yard and installed in 1927. This white screen and the large white pillars adjoining it felt deliciously cool to the touch as the warm day became a hot one and we lingered quite a while as we admired this lovely building.

This church appears to have had more than its fair share of eccentric vicars. One vicar from the 1950's era was upset when he first came to preach there, as there was nowhere to stable his brood mare. His riding boots could be seen under his vestments when he was kneeling during divine service and his groom was expected to have his horse saddled and ready immediately the service was over. I could just imagine him racing down the church aisle, leaping on his horse and galloping headlong down Bourton Hill with his vestments flying in the wind.

We continued on our walk which took us near the Sezincote Estate and eventually were greeted by the astonishing sight of Sezincote House. I had to blink several times to convince myself that I had not suddenly been transported to the Indian sub-continent, for here in the middle of the Cotswolds is a notable example of Neo-Mughal architecture. Who knew that in England we have our very own mini Taj Mahal? This house looked startlingly out of place with its copper onion dome, minarets, pavilions, red sandstone walls and windows that arched into a peacock-like fan.

The house is set in a romantic picturesque-style water garden featuring pools, waterfalls, grottos and a temple to the Hindu Sun God with various life-sized statues of elephants dotted around the grounds.

This house was so eye-poppingly different from the architectural styles of the period in which it was built that we stopped to take lots of pictures. It was then that we noticed visitors paying to take a tour and decided on the spur of the moment to do likewise.

Inside, the architecture and décor followed the same Mughal theme and contrary to my expectations was very pleasing to the eye.

The tour guide was excellent and we learned that Sezincote House was built in 1810 by Charles Cockerell who had worked in India and he was helped by his brother the, architect Samuel Pepys Cockerell, a relative of the diarist Samuel Pepys.

Sezincote House and Gardens takes its name from the independent parish of Sezincote (pronounced See-zin-kt) and is derived from Cheisnecote – 'the home of the oaks' – 'la Chene' being French for an oak tree and 'cot' meaning a dwelling or shelter in Old English. It is not surprising that Sezincote House is reminiscent of the Brighton Pavilion, as it served as this building's inspiration.

My favourite room in Sezincot is the Peacock Bedroom which boasted a four-poster bed that also followed the Mughal-style decoration and is topped with an onion dome decoration. The dining room was wonderful too, spacious with exotic furniture and the walls covered in whimsical murals. Somehow all this works brilliantly with the architecture of the house and I had to revise my purist notion that Palladio-inspired architecture is the best way to go.

I was particularly taken with the semi-circular orangery, which is used nowadays, in addition to nurturing plants, to serve refreshments to the visitors. It is a lovely place to take tea as every few feet there is a 20-foot high window overlooking the lovely Persian Garden of Paradise, featuring fountains and canals. On this occasion, these arched windows were framed by perfectly trimmed jasmine in full bloom which filled the entire orangery with its delicious fragrance.

Although Sezincote House is relatively small by stately home standards and had not taken too long to tour, we now had to make up time so we continued our walk at a smart pace. Just as we were out of puff we encountered the very welcome sight of the Horse and Groom. This pub, which is well-known for its scrumptious food, was buzzing and extremely busy. We had just made it before the heat had wiped us out and were greeted by a very friendly staff who immediately served Randy his choice of a pint of Hook Norton beer while I chugged down a bitter shandy that restored me right away. We were guided over to a menu chalked on a board. It displayed one delicious dish after another. The food is locally sourced and the menu changes frequently. We couldn't choose between Cornish fish soup with rouille, gruyere and crispy toasts, or twice baked goats' cheese with thyme soufflé or spiced roasted carrot with parsnip soup and crème fraîche. Finally, we ordered the Cornish fish soup which was worthy of an haute cuisine restaurant with a top Michelin rating and one of the best we had ever tasted. Other choices included 'Old Spot' pork with chicken and chestnut terrine and homemade piccalilli, and a pancake stuffed with spinach, roast squash, lentil and mascarpone, garnished with a curried sauce.

The entrees provided another dilemma as actually I wanted to try every one of them. There was grilled fillet of Loch Duart salmon, with spinach, brown shrimps and café de Paris butter. Also a roast loin of lamb, with parsnip and Dijon purée and rosemary jus, or a fragrant Massaman lamb curry with steamed jasmine rice and in addition a braised blade of Dexter beef with beetroot and horseradish purée and thyme jus. Any one of these ordered with a sensational side dish of Dauphinoise potatoes is not to be missed.

We shared the unbelievably tasty Cornish fish soup as a starter and I ordered lamb and Randy the Old Spot pork. We chose to eat in the charming, pretty garden at the back of the pub which is terraced with tables on different levels as the ground rises. We sat at a table on the highest terrace and gazed around at the far-reaching views, which gave us a feeling of being on top of the world, as a gentle breeze cooled us.

On the way to our table I had grabbed a newspaper, which the Horse and Groom thoughtfully supplies to customers and an item from it immediately caught my attention. Only the night before we had been watching an episode of our favourite comedy show, *Fawlty Towers*, so I couldn't resist reading out an item from the paper to Randy which could have been a scene from this sitcom. It was reminiscent of the episode in which Basil Fawlty, incandescent with anger, hilariously thrashed his malfunctioning car with a tree branch.

A headmaster of a primary school in Kent, so the paper said, had a similar melt-down. This headmaster's pupils watched open-mouthed as he 'snapped' when the electronic organ he was trying to play refused to work. Enraged, he smashed the keyboard, before wrenching it off its stand and ordering his pupils to follow him as he stormed outside.

In the school grounds the 49-year-old headmaster smashed and stomped on the instrument again – before leaping into his car and repeatedly driving over it. He is now on leave

As I finished reading, a waiter brought a dessert menu. We couldn't manage another morsel but enjoyed reading the selection offered, which including mouth-watering choices of panna cotta with pomegranate and cranberry jelly and spiced clementines or vanilla crème brûlée with pistachio biscotti or apple, pear and cinnamon flapjack crumble.

Our table was the highest in the terrace garden, in front of a drystone wall, and during lunch we gradually became aware of some work being done behind this wall, on the adjoining piece of land. I looked over and realised that an archaeology dig was in progress.

"It's going to be the new car park," said the archaeologist when I inquired, "but, we're near Longborough so it triggered a dig. There's been some great finds already, and we're far from finished."

Apparently, this piece of land belonged to the owners of the Horse and Groom and planning permission had been obtained by them to build a second car park to augment the small one next to the pub. Permission had been granted provided an archaeology survey could be carried out first by the planning authorities. We chatted with the archaeologists, and after finishing lunch we walked around, entered the field and were fascinated to see some of the interesting finds. Medieval walls were beginning to appear and an important site was being revealed. This was great news but although the owners of the Horse and Groom, Tom and Will Greenstock, were also excited by these finds they hadn't anticipated that their car park would have to be placed on hold for quite such a long time as now the site would have to be fully excavated.

It turned out that we had seen the very beginning of the dig and subsequently this small piece of land became the subject of a national news story. The site is believed to have once been a farm complex with ten rooms built around a courtyard and was apparently an 'unusual example of a medieval settlement'.

After nearly three months of digging, the team uncovered another very unusual find, a male human skeleton, thought to date from the late Iron Age and to have had a full ritual burial, which was very rare for this era.

News of the discovery spread, and national interest led to an open day to view the dig and the finds that were excavated. Close to 200 people attended, including a school field trip in addition to members of the Bourton Historical Society.

Cornelius Barton, fieldwork manager at LP Archeology who supervised the dig said, "It is unusual, people did not get buried like this in the Iron Age. Also, there is a structured building probably belonging to a sheep farmer and the remains of a sheepskin coat indicating that this was a sheep farm complex."

The Iron Age skeleton that was found has been nicknamed 'Rusty' by the patrons of the Horse and Groom and it is expected to be displayed at the Corinium Museum in Cirencester.

The findings in the Horse and Groom car park were not quite up there with the news of King Richard III's remains having been found recently under a council car park in Leicester, leading to headlines around the world and a re-evaluation of the character of this king. With this find, further headlines were subsequently generated with the formal burial of King Richard at Leicester Cathedral at which an oration was delivered by Benedict Cumberbatch, of the television series *Sherlock*, who portrays Richard III in a film of the same name. Although Rusty the Iron Age Man did not generate international headlines he certainly caused plenty of excitement, and we were fascinated.

Much as I was interested in the archaeological finds at the Horse and Groom I became rather apprehensive when I discovered from a member of the staff of the pub that all the costs of an archaeology dig have to be paid for by the landowner. Where would we be if something similar was discovered on our land? The Horse and Groom had been flagged for a survey because it was near Longborough, known for its archaeological sites but I had no idea if our cottage was near anything similar. I worried that something like this could really turn into a money pit and be way beyond our budget.

The Horse and Groom had to pay all the costs of the long archaeology dig and during this time building costs skyrocketed and finally the construction of the car park had to be put on hold for the time being until more money could be found to finance the increased costs.

This gave me a lot to think about as we finished our lunch that day and set off for my radio interview in Chipping Campden a few miles away.

The interview was a lot of fun and I was asked to talk about my favourite part of launching my last book, *Cotswolds Memoir*. I talked about the totally unexpected pleasure that publishing my book had brought me – that of meeting my readers. To get the word out about my book I had scheduled a series of book signings and talks and I found I really enjoyed doing this because it connected me with my book buyers.

I did book signings at many independent bookshops in the Cotswolds and I had also been invited to do a series of book signings at numerous branches of Waterstones.

I devised a plan to make contact with my potential readers in an unusual way. I had the cover of my book printed onto a T-shirt, which I wore with a name tag pinned to it. However, instead of my name this name tag bore the message 'I am the author of Cotswolds Memoir... please speak to me, I'm lonely'. Readers would laugh and this would break the ice.

Often my husband Randy would be on hand and as book buyers entered the store he would ask, "Have you met the author?" as if he were at a cocktail party introducing the guest of honour. Then he would bring over the book buyer to be introduced to me. Most people were charmed by my husband's courtly manners. But on one occasion this introduction led to a slight difficulty when Randy introduced me to one particularly assertive elderly lady and left me to chat with her. As Randy walked away to get some coffee she demanded "Where's he going?" in a voice that would have done Maggie Thatcher credit at a political rally. "To get some coffee," I replied. "But I want *him* – I'm not going to be deserted like this!"

"Well, actually I'm the author," I replied, cowering in fear that I was about to be hand-bagged.

"I don't care," she thundered, causing everybody in the book store to turn her way. "I won't be fobbed off with you."

Randy had to be brought back to describe my book and smooth the ruffled feathers.

This story seemed to go over well in the radio interview as it got some laughs from the studio engineer. As the radio station was situated on the High Street of Chipping Campden this provided the ideal opportunity to explore this town once the radio interview was finished.

The Cotswold stone buildings here are a particularly gorgeous colour and every one of them on the main street is awash with a warm honey-hued glow. This creates a flattering haze of colour, a bit like 'the golden hour' as it is known in movie making. The hour before sunset, the cinematographers say, is the best light in which to film. Everybody looks flatteringly lightly tanned as the sunshine bounces this colour off the buildings. The rich tint of this oolitic limestone also seemed to create a mellow mood, as everybody walked around with smiles and was incredibly friendly and helpful.

Chipping Campden is a charming mix of tea shops, boutiques, locally sourced grocery shops, specialist stores, pubs, restaurants and historic sites.

The town was built between the 14th and 17th centuries and we were impressed with the market hall with its magnificent arches and rough cobbled floor, built in 1627.

Sir Baptist Hicks, a rich local silk merchant, had a lot to do with the prosperity of Chipping Campden. He built Campden House, which sadly burned to the ground during the Civil War. It is thought it was torched to prevent it being seized by the Parliamentarians. All that is left of the large estate are two gatehouses, two

Jacobean banqueting houses and Lady Juliana's gateway.

We strolled over to explore the church which looks very grand with its soaring tower and avenue of lime trees leading to the South Porch.

Because Chipping Campden was a prosperous wool trading centre in the Middle Ages, this fine perpendicular church of St. James, built in 1500, is particularly splendid with its medieval altar frontals and interesting Muniment room.

Next, we walked along Church Street until it met the High Street, as I particularly wanted to visit the unusual, almost hidden, Ernest Wilson Garden. After a bit of a search it was found. A small open door marks the entrance to this pretty walled garden and it is easy to miss. It is dedicated to the memory of naturalist 'Chinese' Wilson, as he became known, who set off for China in 1899, at the behest of James Veitch, the celebrated nurseryman of the Royal Botanical Gardens at Kew, to bring back plants.

We were delighted to find this tranquil oasis in the middle of bustling Chipping Campden. It is a good place for visitors to take a rest and admire the exotic plants, which are so different from those in an English garden. We were amazed at how this garden achieved such a feeling of elegance and serenity. There were gorgeous magnolias with an intoxicating perfume, fragrant lilies, the white blossomed *Hydrangea aspera* and the fabulous handkerchief tree, one of Wilson's most exciting discoveries. Wilson introduced around 1,200 species of trees and shrubs to England and wrote several books on his travels including *A Naturalist in Western China*.

The Ernest Wilson Garden can be found on Leysbourne, an extension of the High Street, behind the church. Although this garden is not large it is one of those must-see secret treasures that is not to be missed.

On the way home we took a small detour, a couple of miles away, to the nearby, off-the-beaten-track village of Ebrington, as my research had shown that there were some gorgeous 16th century thatched cottages there. When we arrived and walked around this village's narrow, picturesque streets, we were surprised at the number and perfect beauty of these cottages. Visitors to nearby Hidcote or Kiftsgate Gardens would do well to drive the short distance to Ebrington for fabulous photo opportunities of these historic houses. There is a 14th century manor house in Ebrington, once owned by the Fortescue family and the ancient Norman church of St. Eadburgha, which is filled with many monuments to them.

"Look," said Randy, as he waved a sheaf of paperwork.

A copy of the application for planning permission that Mr T had sent to the council. He threw the papers down on the table and whirled me around in our postage stamp of a living room.

"It's all going to work out," he said, "as soon as we get permission we can start."

"How long will that be, do you think?" I asked.

"Remember Mr T thought it would be about a month and then we are off to the races."

Randy danced us happily into the kitchen as I imagined all the dinner parties we could give when we had enough room.

Five

A LOT MORE OF DOWNTON
Swinbrook, Cogges, Great Coxwell

"Oh no, I don't believe it!" exclaimed Randy. It was about a month after our joyous dance around the living room and he had just answered the telephone.

"But you said it wouldn't be a problem. What happened?"

A cold chill ran down my spine as I realised that Randy must be talking to the architectural planner.

"Are you sure our planning permission for the extension has been denied?"

I sat down in complete shock.

"Is there archaeology under the house?" I asked.

Our application had not been denied because it triggered an archaeology excavation. This was one small consolation at least.

Apparently, the application had been turned down because a window in the design overlooked another property and there had been a complaint by a neighbour and, in addition, there were several other factors.

Why hadn't the architectural planner known that there could be problems? I had trusted his breezy self-confidence. This had turned out to be a mistake. Perhaps he was competent but not with getting listed building permission.

We were really upset as we had asked him to take the utmost care and would be really stretched to find the extra time and money to submit another application. Although Mr T offered to resubmit the application we had lost all faith in him and, difficult as it might be, wanted to hire someone else.

After we had calmed down we decided that not enough research had been done and also that we had accepted the recommendation of Mr T without question from our friends. I am sure they had believed he was the best there was but there was more to it all than anybody knew. It had now become obvious that a better education about the whole process was in order.

We got on the Internet right away. Randy read up on the building process while I visited a number of forums on the subject of acquiring listed building planning permission.

The more I read about listed owners' problems on these forums the more I realised the enormity of what we had taken on. I had not taken action when Mrs Murgatroyd had asked if we knew what we were getting into and on reflection there had been a number of other warnings that had been pushed away. Also, I realised I had been lulled into complacency by the fact that the previous owners had been granted planning permission for an extension on Wisteria Cottage. The fact that the plans had now changed and several years had passed since that permission had been granted had not been seen as potential problems.

As I read on the Internet about other listed property owners' many struggles my anxieties grew. One planning authority was demanding that a home owner near Chipping Campden immediately pull down his entire newly-constructed house. True, the owner had added on more rooms than he had been given permission to build, but even so, this showed the power that the councils had.

Another planning authority in Oldham was demanding that a young family apply for planning permission for the little Wendy playhouse they had put in the garden for their daughter!

Next, I found to my alarm that the planning authorities can take even longer than the month we had waited for our result. Two months is possible and if there are complications permission can take up to six months.

There were several owners who wrote about running out of money in the waiting time needed to make several applications before permission was granted. The terrible word 'bankruptcy' was mentioned in several cases.

I started shivering again. What had we done? Would we end up bankrupt?

Our financial security depended on us getting the cottage fixed up so that we could still work in it while we were staying there and rent it out when we were away.

We could let it out as it stood but the postage stamp living room and the Alice in Wonderland low height door to the en-suite bathroom would turn away a lot of potential tenants. Even if we found a tenant who was willing to put up with the drawbacks these factors would substantially reduce the amount of rent we could obtain. In that case, the low rent would go nowhere near covering the outgoings.

There had to be some help out there somewhere. I put on a big woolly cardigan, and thinking of my mother made a pot of strong tea and spent another couple of hours on the Internet. As I was about to give up I came across The Listed Property Owners' Club. This club had been specifically formed to help the owners of listed buildings overcome obstacles that crop up in obtaining planning permission. Just what I needed.

I contacted the club, which is located in Kent (see contact info at the end of this narrative).

"Most people find us when they are already in trouble and it sounds as if you are. We are happy to help and have experts who can advise you," said a reassuring staff member. We joined gratefully for a relatively low fee.

This club was started over 20 years ago by Peter Anslow, who learned a tremendous amount about owning a listed building after buying a 17th century Kentish barn in the 1960s (which is still being lovingly restored to this day!).

"Any problems that arise with owning a listed building have been, without exception, due to lack of knowledge and it was on this basis that we structured the club," Peter said.

"There aren't many questions that arise that we haven't experienced before. Specialist advice is all part of the membership fee."

A consultation with the club revealed the litany of mistakes we had made. Apparently, our first one was to hire an architectural planner who, in fact, was not an architect. Not only was he not an architect but, as mentioned, he did not specialise in making applications for period properties. There are many nuances involved and a good deal of experience in dealing with the planning authorities regarding period houses makes an enormous difference to the success or failure of an application. There were all kinds of things we should have done ourselves, one of which was to talk to our neighbours and describe what we planned to do and get them on our side. We discovered too that a number of factions have input into the planning process, in addition to a planning committee, including neighbours and town councillors.

We were advised to go back to square one and hire an architect. The club offered a list of architects who specialise in dealing with listed properties. In many cases they have an established relationship with conservation officers, planning committees and local councils. These architects are familiar with all the obstacles in the way of getting permission granted and how to overcome them. In addition, if things become complicated the club can also recommend their specialised legal help.

On the one hand it was an enormous relief to have found this club, on the other the financial implications of starting back at square one were frightening.

When we had a talk about it Randy and I realised, with this new crisis, the funds we had allocated for the building of the extension were just not sufficient. Even the amount I had raised recently, the loan against the film contract for using our cottage as a location, might turn out to be a drop in the ocean now and some drastic measures were needed to keep us solvent. As wonderful as it was to have the support of the Listed Property Owners' Club it was becoming clear that we were by no means out of the woods yet.

After much discussion it seemed the best plan was for me to go back to Los Angeles and for Randy to stay in the Cotswolds. I had an idea for getting work by booking talks through a speakers' agency and also to try for some cartoon work that was still in production during the summer.

Randy meanwhile would stay in the Cotswolds and deal with our crisis. There was the possibility of him bringing in some money at the same time. In Los Angeles, shortly before we had arrived, Randy had worked on the first season of a children's cartoon series which had since aired and done well. Now more episodes had been ordered. If he could get the production company to agree to him recording his role while he was still in England and sending it back to the producers in Los Angeles he would have employment. He planned to rig up a temporary small recording studio in the postage stamp living room. This would mean having nowhere to relax but there wasn't any time for that anyway. At least this way Randy would be on hand to deal with problems that may come up with the extension, and in between record the cartoon episodes and do some building work on the cottage to lay off some of the costs.

The cartoon producers quickly gave the go ahead and we decided to move forward with our plan. It would mean being separated, which we really didn't like at all, but it was the only solution we could see to getting some more money coming through the door in a hurry.

With this plan in place the next order of business was to engage an architect from the Listed Property Owners' Club list. Here we found one, who only wanted to be referred to as Mr A (for architect). He suggested that we would save time and money in the long run if we did things properly this time. He advised us to hire a project manager, even though Randy had considered taking this on himself. Although we blanched at the cost we agreed. We would have to find the money somehow. He ordered a new survey and from this his quantum surveyor gave us a more accurate estimate of what the extension would cost. Again, it was a shock but we were in this so deep that there seemed to be no alternative but to move forward.

As Mr A specialised in working on listed buildings he knew exactly what caused applications for planning permission to be turned down.

As Mr A worked on our plans he found ways of following the rules and at the same time still coming up with ingenious ways of giving us what we wanted in the design of the extension.

Mr A said, "There will, no doubt, have to be some informal negotiations behind the scenes with the planning authorities which I will carry out. I will also set up a site meeting with the conservation officer and I'll get you as much as I possibly can of what you want."

As he continued he educated us a little.

"Do bear in mind that conservationists and planners are not there to make your life a misery, they are trying to protect the environment.

"One of the reasons you chose this property is most likely because all the buildings around your cottage look almost as they did four or five hundred years ago. You can see what a good job the conservationists have been doing, not just here but all over Britain. We need to strike a balance between the needs of modern life and the preservation of your fine period property. What is best is to work with the planners and not make it difficult for them."

As he walked around our cottage he also pointed out a number of things to look out for as the building work progressed.

"See that," he said pointing to a partially rotted out beam. "It's oak and it's mandatory, if permission is granted, for that to be replaced with oak and no other wood." He continued on with several other examples of 'like for like' replacements.

Then he took us outside.

"Owners don't realise," he said, "that the listed building regulations apply not just to the building in question but to the entire property, including garden features, gates and outbuildings. If any of the outbuildings collapsed during rebuilding, permission would not be granted to rebuild. Permission would only be granted on renovating existing structures."

There was a lot more of this and I tried to take it in, but after a while my brain began to fuse. I just tuned out and thanked my lucky stars that I had found the Listed Property Owners' Club.

Once we had settled on the design of the extension the next stage was to have the plans finalised, and while this went ahead Mr A made it clear that we needed to do our part too, which was to primarily get our neighbours on our side. We knew a number of people in the village through renting holiday accommodation from Mrs M before we bought Wisteria Cottage. Mrs M's village is only two miles away so there was a lot of overlap with the social life of the two villages. However, there were a couple of immediate neighbours that we had not met.

We introduced ourselves to these neighbours, including the couple that had played a part in our failed planning permission attempt and invited them all over to our cottage to show them our renovation plans.

A tasty spread of home cooked tapas, prosecco and elderflower cordial was laid out before them as we asked for their input.

This led to lots of lively discussion and ideas. The food and wine was a big success and by the end of the evening everybody had bonded and seemed interested in being as cooperative as possible.

After this I turned my attention back to my money-making scheme of producing a talk about the *Downton Abbey* film locations in the Cotswolds.

My recent visit to Bampton had given me the idea of producing this talk as the history of the buildings and villages used for the scenes in Downton is fascinating, and describing it in my talk would add, I thought, even more interest and enjoyment to viewers of this series.

I realised that for those Americans who could not make the trip to England, a talk on *Downton Abbey*'s location shooting in the Cotswolds might be a popular draw if I were to be engaged for a programme of these in the USA.

I got on the phone to several agencies in Los Angeles that arranged speaking engagements and pitched my 'Downton Abbey in the Cotswolds' idea.

As I waited to hear if these agencies could sell my talk I assembled photos, video clips and historical material from my previous visit to Bampton. Now I needed material for all the other locations and Randy and I moved on to explore *Downton Abbey*'s location in Swinbrook.

The Swan Inn at Swinbrook near Burford in Oxfordshire was used in the scenes portraying the love nest of Lady Sybil and Branson the chauffeur during their elopement in the second series of *Downton Abbey* and is situated on the south side of the village.

The astonishing beauty of this location, with the picturesque Swan Inn swathed in wisteria and perched next to an ancient bridge on the River Windrush is truly magical.

This boutique inn was owned by one of the Mitford sisters, the Dowager Duchess of Devonshire, or Debo as she was known to her family, and is now maintained by her estate. The Mitford family grew up in Swinbrook and nearby Asthall and a visit to this inn and the village of Swinbrook will instantly recall, to viewers of the series, the scenes in *Downton Abbey* which were filmed there.

Inside is an unbelievably cosy collection of small bars and dining rooms, each decorated with very large, fascinating old photographs featuring the Mitford family, made famous and also often notorious by the antics and talent of the their six daughters. The Mitford sisters, during their heyday in the 1920s and 1930s, had their portraits drawn by William Acton, and copies of these form the centrepiece of the images on the walls of the inn. They hang over a fireplace in one of the front dining rooms and show Nancy the novelist, who wrote in Paris, Debo who became the Duchess of Devonshire, Jessica a communist and a writer of best-selling non-fiction, Unity, notorious for being a Fascist and friend of Hitler, Diana also a Fascist and married to Oswald Mosley, and Pam who was content to look after her farm.

Nancy's novel *The Pursuit of Love* and Jessica's fascinating memoir *Hons and Rebs* are excellent reads for those who wish to immerse themselves in the Mitford saga. These books chronicle the often hilariously eccentric English family life of this era. The Mitford sisters' father, Lord Redesdale, among many other odd pastimes, often indulged in one of his favourite sports the 'child hunt'. When no foxes were to hand he would, instead, chase his children through the countryside on horseback with his bloodhounds in hot pursuit.

A country garden at the back of the inn, overlooking a field dotted with sheep, is ideal for lunch or a drink before dinner. All who lunch or dine here are enchanted by the chickens and roosters clucking and cock-a-doodle-dooing as they peck and prance around the tables.

There are eleven bedrooms at the inn with evocative names, which no doubt refer to their earlier use, such as The Forge, Orchard Store and Piggery End. Debo's Room is the best, with its enormous roll top bath and exposed beams. The rooms are designer-elegant with just the right amount of rustic charm, retaining all of the original character of these ancient buildings.

Archie and Nicola Orr-Ewing who run the inn get full marks for cuisine along with all else and serve up a drool-worthy selection of locally-sourced produce. In addition, there is prime Hereford beef from Bledington, lamb and poultry from Aubrey Allen and cheese from Fromage to Age. Don't miss the kippers for breakfast, or for dinner the duck pâté, Fowey mussels and gloriously yummy baked ginger pudding.

There are still more delights, not least of which is a stroll through the sleepy stone-walled village of Swinbrook, described by Jessica Mitford as 'a dozen grey cottages huddled like Cotswold sheep'. There is a tiny green in front of the village hall, a well-used cricket pitch complete with an old-fashioned wooden pavilion and a pretty church, the interior of which is a must-see.

St. Mary's Church of the Virgin is famous for its startling, recumbent marble effigies. Here, wall tombs contain six life-sized marble likenesses of the male line of the Fettiplace family who owned all the surrounding land for over four centuries. This family commissioned the marble effigies for the church beginning in the 17th century and they are to be found in the sanctuary and the choir. They are stacked one on top of another on marble shelves, almost as if reclining in couchettes on the Orient Express. Some are gilded and propped up on one elbow, portrayed fully-dressed, wearing late Tudor-style armour with swords, gauntlets, lace jabots and sporting, in some cases, luxuriant, shoulder length, curly hair.

Do not miss in the chancel the five cartoonishly grotesque and amusing misericords carved into the choir stalls which portray a lion, two men weaving and a woman spinning wool.

There is so much of interest in Swinbrook for *Downton Abbey* fans in addition, as they will no doubt agree, to being the best choice for this series' most romantic storyline.

After exploring Swinbrook and having dinner at the excellent Swan Inn, Randy and I discussed how much the cuisine and service in the Cotswolds had improved and was now easily comparable with top London and French restaurants. The improvement has been dramatic, and as we talked we remembered our experience of only a handful of years ago in a little café in the Cotswolds (that has since gone out of business) whose service was so bad that we laughed about it.

I reminded Randy of the time he ordered breakfast in this café and asked for his egg to be flipped over. The waitress looked around the empty restaurant like John Inman in *Are You Being Served* when asked if he was free and said, "No, we're very busy and the cook doesn't have time for special orders."

This same waitress came to collect our plates after we had finished the meal.

"You haven't eaten your beans," she said accusingly.

"No," said Randy, "I don't want them."

"But that's your protein," she protested. "I'll still have to charge you for them. It's no good asking me to take them off the bill."

"I wasn't," said Randy.

Not listening, she raised her voice.

"I won't do it!" We looked on astounded as she instantly worked herself up to a fever pitch

"You customers expect me to change all the rules and here I am run off my feet." She seemed oblivious of the fact that there was still nobody in the café but us and became incoherent with rage before finally throwing the bill at us. We had such a good laugh at this that we gratefully left her quite a large tip.

I remembered another occasion, several years ago, when a promising looking restaurant in the Cotswolds quickly dropped in my estimation when I asked for a glass of water. The waitress replied, "No, I can't get you one because if I do that means I will have to bring one to anybody else who asks."

On another occasion at another restaurant in the Cotswolds my mother and I were handed a huge menu with dozens of choices. The waitress stood by as we studied it. We couldn't believe our luck, and after much pondering over the embarrassment of riches offered finally decided to splurge on Lobster thermidor and coq au vin. When we told the waitress our choices she replied

"Tonight we've only got steak and kidney pie or fish and chips."

Randy matched this with his experience in a café in America when he had ordered breakfast. It arrived absolutely stone cold.

When he complained, the waitress slapped her grubby hand down on his bacon and eggs and had a good feel of the whole mess before replying.

"You're darn tootin' honey, cold as ice."

The next day, as I was putting together my research on Swinbrook, a call came from Los Angeles telling me my pitch had gone over so well that several talks on *Downton Abbey*'s locations in the Cotswolds had been booked immediately.

With this news I arranged my airline ticket for Los Angeles.

Next, Randy and I set off to visit the *Downton Abbey* film location, Cogges, near Witney in Oxfordshire.

Cogges Manor Farm is transformed into *Downton Abbey*'s Yew Tree Farm for the farm scenes portrayed in the fourth and several subsequent seasons.

It is the home of Mr Drewe, the tenant farmer, and there are many scenes shot around the farm buildings and in the manor farm house's interior. It is here that Marigold, Lady Edith's illegitimate daughter is raised.

Apparently, the location manager for *Downton Abbey* was in Bampton during the filming of one of the earlier episodes and about to begin his search for a suitable farm for these scenes with Lady Edith. He asked Bampton's butcher if he knew of one. When he was directed to Cogges Manor Farm he couldn't believe his luck and literally skipped with joy as he saw that nothing in the manor house's interior had been changed in well over a hundred years. Also, the manor house is surrounded by numerous historic farm buildings making this the perfect location with only a minimal need for set dressing.

Randy and I wanted first to find what was left of the village of Cogges, which was incorporated into Whitney in 1932, and discovered that all that remains is the Church of St. Mary, the former Vicarage and Cogges Manor Farm.

We strolled around the church, which is awkwardly scrunched between other buildings, and took photos of its decorated Gothic windows. The church of St. Mary's originated in the 12th century and is a mixture of Norman and Saxon architecture with some Romanesque walls.

Cogges village is mentioned in the Domesday Book which shows that by 1086 a water mill had been established, most likely on the nearby River Windrush.

Cogges is an important heritage site, on which a priory, traces of a large manor house and a medieval village have been found. All that remains easily visible are parts of a defensive moat.

On entering Cogges Manor Farm we were amazed at the beauty of the well-preserved farm buildings, which included an ox byre, wheat and barley barns, pig sties and a dairy. We paid for our tickets in the lovely old dairy barn, cow stalls still in place, and now used as a café and shop. The beams were so low that Randy had to stoop to avoid hitting his head.

This site is also a popular attraction for families and it was fun to see young children discovering the various animals that are dotted around the farm yard.

Pygmy goats, Oxford Sandy and black pigs, Lleyn sheep from North Wales, chickens, ducks and rabbits were among the many animals causing squeals of delight from children as they ran around the interesting collection of historic barns and farm buildings.

There is a picnic lawn, an adventure play area and all manner of other activities, making this a great day out all round.

My eye was immediately drawn to the manor house, frequently used as a farmhouse over the centuries, where many of the scenes from the Cotswolds location of *Downton Abbey* were shot. One wing of this building is mid-12th century and a second wing was added in 1667.

In 1974 Oxfordshire County Council bought this manor and the farm and converted it into Cogges Manor Farm Museum.

Upon entering the kitchen of the manor house we realised that the set dressers on *Downton Abbey* had indeed done almost nothing, merely supplying some kitchen utensils and a few other small changes. The clock had stopped in this room in 1895 and it was like stepping through a time portal. It was fascinating to actually be on the film set where Lady Edith had visited little Marigold.

Nothing is roped off and there is complete access to the kitchen as it is shown on the screen. We couldn't believe that it had been so well preserved. Not only was there the typical cast-iron kitchen range of the day which servants were required to blacken and polish every morning, but the furniture, the paint colours and floor were perfectly in period too.

We sat down at the kitchen table, absorbed the atmosphere and tried to imagine what it would have been like to live in those times.

Next, we explored several other fascinating rooms in the manor house. There was the back kitchen which features a large copper used for washing clothes and a bread oven which is built into the thickness of the wall. In addition there was the pantry which was used to store food, before refrigeration, and next door the cold room which is partly below ground and featured a meat safe and barrels for home-made cider and beer. The dairy, on the other side of the house, with its medieval floor, contains all that was used during that era for butter churning and cheese production.

A room known as William Blake's study in the manor house is now designated as a dress-up room for fans of *Downton Abbey*. There is a rack of period clothes for both adults and children, along with a pile of hats. Once dressed it is possible to take photographs in the kitchen 'set' and look like a character who has appeared in *Downton Abbey*.

As I was looking at the rack of clothes in this room, two children, accompanied by their grandmother, were having lots of fun dressing up in clothes from the Downton era.

I gathered a useful amount of material here for my talk and we moved on to another location that, thanks to the magic of television editing, appears to be part of this farm in *Downton Abbey* but is, in fact, several miles away.

In the care of the National Trust, the Great Barn in Great Coxwell village is an incredibly impressive example of the skills of medieval carpenters and the vast wealth of the monasteries.

This barn's sheer size was enough to make us gasp and the beauty of its craftsmanship inspires complete awe.

This barn is the only surviving building of a once prosperous 13th century grange that provided income to Beaulieu Abbey, and although technically in the Vale of the Whitehorse, in Oxfordshire, it could perhaps qualify as 'Cotswolds' because it is constructed of Cotswolds rubble-stone walling.

This barn, with its massive wooden beams that support the roof, also impressed the designer William Morris who described it as 'unapproachable in its dignity'. This grange would have been surrounded by a windmill, pig farm and dairy herd, all now gone. However, with *Downton Abbey*'s filming, several of these missing elements are now supplied, on screen, by Cogges Manor Farm.

We walked around the charming village of Great Coxwell, right by the barn, admiring its neat thatched cottages, and visited the church of St. Giles, parts of which date from the 13th century. It is situated on a ridge on the south side of the village and its churchyard is now a wildlife area which features over a hundred species of wildflowers.

We hurried on as I wanted to photograph the *Downton Abbey* location in Shilton, a pretty village two miles south of Burford in Oxfordshire, which I describe in my earlier book, *Cotswolds Memoir*.

This village has a ford across a picturesque brook and beside it is The Old Forge, which became The Red Lion public house for the filming. This is where Mr Bates found employment after he left Downton Abbey in the second season. Directly across from the brook is an 18th century hump-backed bridge which is also featured in this segment of the filming.

Invited by a friend, I had been lucky enough to fleetingly attend the wrap party for the last of the filming in Bampton of the *Downton Abbey* series and was able to include some personal anecdotes. The party was held in Sandford Field on the outskirts of Bampton and was a very informal barbeque with draft beer and other drinks served by members of the cast.

Hugh Bonneville, who plays Lord Grantham in the series was serving pints to the guests and happily posing with all who requested a photo. He also posed for photos with Alan Leech, who plays Tom Branson.

Samantha Bond, who plays Lady Rosamund Painswick, chatted to all of us, as did Kevin Doyle who plays Mr Moseley. It was fun to meet these actors and other members of the cast and they were all very personable and friendly, posing for photographs and giving autographs all evening long, as they said thank you and goodbye to all in Bampton.

Back in Wisteria Cottage, Randy and I worked hard to pull all the material we had gathered into my talk. Randy dove-tailed his still photos and video segments into my personal anecdotes about cast members and the filming, together with my descriptions of the history and architecture of buildings used in the *Downton Abbey* series in the Cotswolds.

Just as we finished there was a flurry of activity on the cottage extension. Mr A's latest site meeting with the conservation officer had resulted in a small tussle that could have caused a bit of a hitch. We wanted to take down the wall between the two tiny guest bedrooms to make one decent-sized room. At first the conservation officer had indicated that this would not fly. But then Mr A had been able to prove that these two rooms had originally been built as one.

We were overjoyed, as the two rooms at present would only accommodate a single bed. Now, when this was renovated we could have a proper guest bedroom. Mr A did well to win this argument but compromise was needed on a several other things. The window that overlooked the neighbour's property was put in a different position and the bathroom that was to go into the structure to join up the cart shed/living room with the cottage had to be made smaller. Some of the materials we wanted to use had to change too.

Mr A was meticulous and got everything sorted out to do with permissions. Only then did he draw up the plans to finish the application and submit it to the council.

Now the application had to go before the planning committee to see if permission would be granted.

All too soon it was time for a farewell dinner before taking my flight to Hollywood. This dinner doubled as a birthday celebration for Randy, and together with our friends, we set off for Prithvi Fine Dining Indian Restaurant in Cheltenham.

This was an extraordinary experience, delicious, and like no other Indian meal I had ever had. The taster's menu was decided on by all at the table and it did not disappoint. Each course was accompanied by a wine that was especially selected by the restaurant's sommelier to complement the meal and it certainly did.

Mint coriander chicken with chilli chutney and quail egg with a Sauvignon Blanc from Tasmania were paired for one of the courses and the result was exquisite.

For the next course I substituted the seabass, with salmon, mussels, white wine vinegar and sun dried chilli which was out of this world. Course after course appeared, making a total of five, each more subtly nuanced and tasty than the last.

Despite the fact that the courses were not large the careful choice of ingredients meant that we were perfectly satisfied at the end of the meal. We did not feel we had over-eaten even though the dessert was salted caramel chocolate with pistachio, served with orange Muscat and Flora wine.

This is a wonderful restaurant, particularly for a special occasion, as the food is sensational, the ambiance simple and elegant with plain, pale walls and tablecloths. The white glove service is rather posh and amazingly good. Everything is explained on the taster's menu including the reason for choosing the particular wine that is offered.

We had some good laughs with our friends and Randy enjoyed his musical birthday cards. It was the perfect get together. The next day I said goodbye with a heavy heart as I climbed on an airplane bound for Hollywood. I was somewhat apprehensive at our separation and also about my ability to raise more funds for the extension to the cottage. By the time dear little England was disappearing below me into the distance, looking smaller and smaller through the airplane's window, I had already blubbed my way through an entire box of tissues.

Clockwise from Top: Downton Abbey wrap party, Sandford Field, Bampton. Hugh Bonneville (Lord Grantham), Allen Leech (Tom Branson) and Samantha Bond (Lady Rosamund Painswick).

Clockwise from Top: Downton War Memorial in Bampton. Isobel Crawley's house.
Bampton Library (Downton Hospital). Downton extras. *Opposite, Clockwise from Top*
Penelope Wilton (Isobel Crawley), Maggi Smith (Violet Crawley).
Photo: James Wildman. Michael Fox (Andy Parker), Rob James-Collier (Thomas
Barrow).Photo James Wildman. Downton Abbey pub in Bampton.

THE SWAN IN

Top: The Swan Inn at Swinbrook. The love nest of Lady Sybil and Branson in Downton Abbey. *Below*: Great Coxwell Barn used in Yew Tree Farm scenes. *Opposite, Clockwise from Top*: Laura Carmichael (Lady Edith Crawley) and Michelle Dockery (Lady Mary Crawley) in Downton. Photo: James Wildman. Cogges Farm location for Yew Tree Farm. Kitchen of Cogges Farm.

Clockwise from top: Jim Carter (Mr. Carson). Photo: James Wildman. Grantham A[...] in Church View, Bampton. St. Mary of the Virgin, Bampton used as Downton's chu[...] Vintage car used in Downton's filming. Opposite: Uley Bury, Gloucestershire.

Warwick Castle, Warwickshire
Opposite: Westwell Garden, Oxfordshire on National Garden Scheme open day.

Above: Garden Seat at Wisteria Cottage
Opposite: Stowell Park on National Garden Scheme Open Day

TEAS IN
BALLROOM

Above: Wisteria outside the Lamb Inn, Burford. *Below:* Detail From the door of All Saints Church in Faringdon.
Opposite: Sunset on the Thames over Radcot Bridge.

Above: In Chipping Campden. *Below*: Campden House Gardens.
Opposite Top: Palladian Bridge at Prior Park *Below*: Cornwell Manor, Oxfordshire

Above: Chavenage House Engraving, 1840 *Below*: Chavenage House, Gloucestershi
Opposite: Snowshill Garden- Gloucestershire *Below*: Snowshill Lavender Fields

Above: Rural Skills demonstrated at the Old Prison, Northleach, Gloucestershire
Opposite: Dishes and drinks from the Cotswolds.

Slate-roofed and thatched Cotswold cottages

Six

PLAYING THE WAITING GAME
Church Enstone, Neat Enstone, Fulwell

"I am 'ere for zee audition but I 'ave to meet zee director NOW – I 'ave no time to wait my turn."

The casting assistant was young and eager to please. She meekly said. "I'll go and tell the director right away," and hurried off.

I was having a hectic time in Hollywood. The day after I arrived, and still suffering from jet lag, I presented my first talk on *Downton Abbey* in the Cotswolds and was booked for an audition that required me to speak in a French accent.

Arriving at the audition I realised I would be in competition with native French speakers. To give myself an edge I pretended to be French, even though I only knew a smattering of the language.

I love France but the French can be a little abrasive sometimes so I threw myself into the character of a haughty Parisienne as if I were acting a role in a play. I laid on an incredibly superior, obnoxious attitude and it worked. A few moments later I was beckoned past a group of actresses who had been there before me and into the producer's office. In a voice dripping with contempt I said, "I 'ave no time for zis – I 'ave to read ze part NOW – I have anozzer audition and I cannot be late – it is for a better job zan zis one."

Amazingly, the head of casting jumped up and handed me the script.

I glanced at the first couple of lines and said, "Before I read – I see I 'ave to say ze the name Philip. Do you want me to say it ze correct way – or all wrong like you Americans do? In France ze correct way is Philleep."

"Oh, please say it the French way," the director said, as the producer nodded in agreement.

After I read, the director said, "That was excellent."

Although I was quaking inside – thoughts of the money I needed for my little bit of heaven in the Cotswolds spurred me on to crazy lengths. I looked at my watch,

"Bon. Now do not waste my time – tell me if I 'ave zee job – ozzerwise I may take anozzer job and will not be available." With total conviction I exclaimed, "You will not find anyone better zan me!"

The director turned to his producer and head of casting and whispered, suddenly they were all nodding together.

"Yes, you've got the job," said the producer in a shell-shocked voice.

I couldn't believe it. No one had even asked if I was actually French.

The role was to replace the lead actress's voice in a television series that had been made in Europe. Her French accent was way too thick but, worse, she couldn't act. It meant five full days of work. Then it dawned on me that I was going to have to keep up the charade of being French for the entire length of the job.

It is ironic that often an actor's best work is performed off stage rather than on. This was going to be one of those times.

All was fine until the third day when, on a quick break, I checked my messages and found an urgent call from my agent. There was a terrific hurry to cast a vocal role that required a Cockney accent and, if I wanted the job, I had to do a telephone audition immediately. Only having a minute or so I slipped into an empty office of the recording studio and closed the door. I was just finishing in my best East End street voice when the door opened and there was the director who had come to say the break was over. His puzzled expression showed he was trying to make sense of what he had half-heard as he caught a few words of my Cockney voice. I panicked for a second. Would I be exposed as a fraud and not be paid?

Thinking quickly, I said, "So zorry to keep you waiting – I 'ad to audition for my agent in ze native accent of my region of France... eet zounds so... how you say... like ze

Cockney accent except, but of course, eet is in zee French."

"Oh I see," said director. He stood there trying to put this together with what he had just experienced. He looked as if his head might explode so I rushed back to the studio before he could say anything else.

"Wow," I thought, "that was a close one."

On the last day of work I heaved a sigh of relief as I performed the final line of dialogue. I thought I was home and dry as I heard the welcome words 'It's a wrap'.

But another minefield awaited me. A girlfriend of one of the studio engineers arrived who was (quelle horreur!) from France.

The engineer was standing within earshot of the producer and director, when he introduced me to her. "This is Yvette, would you chat with her in French. She's lonely for someone to talk to in her native tongue."

I think steam came out of my ears as my brain worked at warp speed to figure a way out of this dilemma. Suddenly, something clicked and I turned to her and said, "Oooh I am zo zorry but I am working so 'ard on learning ze English zat I 'ave promised myself I will not speak French because... it makes me forget ze English. I 'ope you understand."

Before she could reply I exclaimed, "Oops look at ze time. I 'ave to go."

Grabbing my things I literally ran out of the studio, jumped in my car and burned rubber out of the car park.

It was all go, as that evening I got an urgent call to fill in for an actress who had dropped out of re-voicing a cable television comedy series.

"I played Polly the potty-mouthed parrot. It was a cable TV show and they had me swearing like a trouper. Can parrots blush?" I was on the telephone to Randy who was laughing at my news. "And what about you?" I continued.

"I was barking into a tea pot in my cartoon series to get the right sound for playing an astronaut dog in a helmet," replied Randy. "Sometimes I can't believe what we do to earn a buck. It's been difficult though, every time I tried to record another voice there would be a loud moo from the cows in the meadow. Can't wait to get our little study office built and make it soundproof. It was kinda funny though, Stockings wouldn't let up. I think she's ready for stardom."

I had a pang of homesickness for the Cotswolds as Randy referred to our favourite cow, whom we had dubbed Stockings, because she is all white except for her legs, which make her look like a black-stockinged can-can dancer.

"Any news?" I asked hopefully. Randy knew what this meant. Had we heard from the architect? When planning permission or refusal comes through the planning officer contacts the home owner's architect directly.

"No, not a word," Randy replied. I moaned in frustration.

"Got a lot of information from The Listed Property Owners' Club today though," he continued. "What a terrific resource this is turning out to be. Well done on finding it."

Although we were still waiting for permission, the club had outlined a number of improvements, permitted by the planners, and Randy could accomplish these in the meantime. This work would certainly help to defray some of the building expenses.

"Just been chipping away at the concrete pointing on the outside walls of the cart shed," he said. The Listed Property Owners' Club had been helping Randy with advice about the concrete that had been used in some of the pointing on the cart shed walls.

Randy explained that this concrete, frequently mistakenly used, is what stops old buildings 'breathing' and causes damp. Once it is cleared out it is best to repoint it with lime mortar. It is time-consuming and tedious but is something that can be done relatively easily by the home owner and saves a lot on labour costs.

The Listed Property Owners' Club had also been helping Randy identify and find suppliers for various building materials that have to be 'like for like' with the original materials used.

Next, I filled Randy in on my news – my first *Downton Abbey* talk had been a big success and the

American fans of the series had so many questions for my Q & A segment afterwards that the session had taken twice as long as usual. These fans couldn't get enough of my personal anecdotes about the location shooting in the Cotswolds and really enjoyed my run-down on the history of the buildings used.

My agency raised my fee and quickly booked more *Downton Abbey* talks. I also had several vocal jobs and worked more or less steadily for two months. I put every penny I could into the bank and so did Randy in England as he continued work on his cartoon series.

Before my trip to Los Angeles I had booked a talk at the Pudding Club in Mikleton, and I wanted to keep my commitment, so after almost three months in America, I returned to the Cotswolds.

"What do you think of that?" asked Randy, indicating the gorgeous view.

"It's stunning," I gasped.

To celebrate my return Randy had taken me to lunch at the Feathered Nest Country Inn near the small village of Nether Westcote, just north of Burford in Oxfordshire.

I had been really missing Randy and the Cotswolds a lot and I couldn't quite believe that we were sitting on the sun-drenched terrace of this lovely inn perched on a hill overlooking a panoramic view of the Evenlode Valley. A perfect Cotswold vista of rolling hills, drystone walls and patchwork-quilted fields stretched into the far distance past the Evenlode to the lush green trees of Wychwood Forest beyond.

The terrace tables at the Feathered Nest are grouped under the spreading boughs of a shady old sycamore tree and an atmosphere of serenity prevailed. It was quiet enough to hear birds sing, as the friendly staff brought delicately flavoured dishes to us. Everything was so perfect, one of those moments that seemed as if it were from a dream.

"What's the matter?" asked my concerned husband.

I was blubbing. Randy handed me a hanky and gave me a hug.

"That view of the Cotswolds, this gorgeous restaurant, I'm so happy to be back," I sobbed, as all my emotions spilled out causing a few people to glance over from another table. I had been working flat out and everything had caught up with me.

Building the extension was turning into just as much of a roller coaster ride as finding the cottage.

"Is it all worth it?" I asked.

"Of course it is. Hang in, it can't be much longer now."

I couldn't stay teary for too long. Having a meal at the Feathered Nest was such a sublime experience. It easily won my vote for the best restaurant I had visited in the entire Cotswolds.

Originally an old malt house, the building in which the Feathered Nest is housed was once part of an enclave of buildings consisting of a coach house, stables, a piggery, and a coal shed and was first documented in 1692.

This multiple award-winning inn has been carefully renovated by Amanda and Tony Timmer and full marks to them for such a tasteful remodel. The décor is extremely attractive with the perfect blend of rustic charm, heritage paint colours, luxurious fabrics, interesting antique pieces dotted around and amusing features such as vintage horse saddles for bar seats. There are several rooms for accommodation at the inn with names such as The Pheasant Nest, the Cuckoo's Den and the Dove Cote making for a very romantic retreat.

The food is amazingly good and good value too, especially at lunch with the set menu and it is, of course, delicious haute cuisine. We heard it whispered that head chef Kuba Winkowski was formerly at Le Manoir, Raymond Blanc's restaurant near Oxford. True or not we liked the food here better and together with his team the Feathered Nest's chef creates exquisitely tasty dishes.

On this occasion I almost swooned over the complex flavours of the king crab apple, lemon verbena, celery, soft shell crab tempura. While Randy was delighted with the Wagyu beef ravioli, with cep mushrooms, parmesan and spinach. I knew I would have been equally 'sent' by the courgette flower with buttermilk curd, pearl millet and vegetable casserole. We shared a dessert of hazelnut with Pedro Ximenez parfait, praline and chocolate and smiled at each other like two Cheshire cats that had just had the cream.

The next day we had another memorable lunch. Mrs Murgatroyd, having heard from Randy that I was returning, invited us to an event that was already arranged with her friends and made it double as a welcome back to me.

We were happy to have another opportunity to spend time in the Murgatroyds' company and a further visit to the rambling old pile of a manor house that appeared to have been forgotten by time.

"Hello, I'm Captain Digby Fortesque. I'm sure I know you?"

At the lunch we were seated next to a charming old boy who was smartly dressed in a blue blazer with brass buttons and a silk cravat.

"Call me Digby. Have you ever been to Mombasa?" continued Captain Fortesque.

Without waiting for an answer he regaled us with stories of his many exploits. We listened enthralled as he barely drew breath between stories, and when we arrived at the cheese and biscuits he launched into a description of his adventures in the secret service. Suddenly, he glanced around in a suspicious manner and lowered his voice to a whisper.

"I've got a tip for you," he advised sagely. "Always a good idea to carry a disguise in case you should need it at a moment's notice."

With that he produced from his pocket a wig, a huge handlebar moustache and thick horn-rimmed spectacles.

"Never without one myself. Dashed handy," he said, as he crouched down below the dining table and donned his disguise. "You see, you can change your appearance in a matter of seconds."

However, when he attempted this, his wig was askew, his moustache fell off immediately and his glasses slipped to the end of his nose. We could hardly contain ourselves as we watched him looking furtively around the room.

"I guarantee you not one person at this lunch will recognise me now," he said, as he popped up above the dining table and his wig slipped even further over one eye.

Another guest exclaimed, "I say, Digby, are you hogging the brandy again? Come on, pass it around."

We seemed to have stepped into a scene from a P.G. Wodehouse story, and this continued after lunch when we progressed to the drawing room where the guests were reunited with their dogs. Astonishingly, everybody there had a shiatsu. None of these guests seemed too steady on their feet and the pack of yapping canines were running amok, trailing leashes, which wrapped around their owners' ankles, and threatened to send half of them crashing to the floor. As the dogs tore around like banshees, knocking the lunch guests off-balance, more and more cups of coffee and glasses of brandy were spilled down shirt fronts and dresses.

We whispered to each other that this party was quite a bit more outrageous than many we had attended in Hollywood.

Mrs Mugatroyd, oblivious to all the mayhem created by the dogs, indicating the two of us, announced, "These guests are very good at impressions and I was hoping they would perform a few for you all." Turning to us she said in a rather flustered manner, "Oh eh... that is not why I invited you, of course."

We think she wanted to show us off as by now we had performed a few more impressions for her and she had finally realised that these were supposed to be funny. She never actually laughed but would say things like 'How clever' and 'Delightful'.

Choosing impressions that we thought the rather elderly lunch guests would relate to we imitated Katharine Hepburn and Ronald Reagan. There was a smattering of applause after our little show and the Brigadier and Mrs M thanked us. The Brigadier soon wandered off and we were left chatting with Mrs M and her friend Imelda. We loved hearing their old stories and, as they were a little tipsy after drinks at lunch, it was easy to get them talking about their past. They giggled like schoolgirls, remembering their days of being courted by different beaus before they were married.

"Of course," said Mrs M, "everything was very innocent in those days. We wouldn't dream of carrying on before marriage."

Imelda joined in. "Goodness me – no. It's so different today. But we were like babes in the wood."

Next, they looked at each other in a meaningful way.

"Well there was an exception," said Imelda.

"Yes," said Mrs M, "and we both know who that was."

Together they exclaimed, "Lavinia!"

Peals of giggles convulsed them before Mrs M continued. "Lavinia did what was forbidden and had... eh... relations... with her beau – who was quite a deal older than her. We couldn't understand how she could, especially as we thought he was revolting."

"He was a politician and very fat," explained Imelda. "When we found out what she had done all the gals crowded around Lavinia and asked her what it was like. 'Awful', she exclaimed!"

More giggles erupted from them both as Mrs M continued.

"Lavinia said, 'It was like having a wardrobe fall on top of you with the key sticking out.'"

The next day, Randy and I set off for my talk and book signing at a literary lunch hosted by the organisers of the Pudding Club at the Three Ways Hotel in Mickleton. This literary lunch is an offshoot of the actual Pudding Club, which has become an institution in the Cotswolds as the mecca of delicious desserts. This club was founded by a small dedicated group of pudding lovers whose mission was to stop the disappearance of traditional British puddings because of the encroachment of convenience food and overseas influences. In 1985, a small band of aficionados, Simon and Jill Coombe and Peter Henderson, with a big assist from Shelia Vincent (The Queen of Puddings), joined together to host regular evenings of indulgence which produced seven delicious puddings. These included British childhood favourites like treacle sponge and jam roly poly in addition to more arcane ones such as Kentish well pudding, apple dappy and Scottish flummery, in addition to many others which at that time were not widely available. The Pudding Club achieved their goal of preserving the Great British Pudding and now many restaurants, pubs, farm shops and supermarkets up and down the country feature these traditional puds.

International visitors come from far and wide and join the locals to enjoy a whole evening's entertainment on Pudding Club meets. A Parade of Puddings is presented and amid much fun, banging of spoons on the dining table, and ceremony, there is a vote for 'best pudding'. Comments from those who have attended these evenings have described them as 'like making love in a thunderstorm' and a 'medieval banquet with custard'.

The literary offshoot of this is an entertaining event eagerly taken up by the 'ladies who lunch' set, where a delicious lunch is served with, of course, a wonderful pudding followed by a talk given by the author of a newly-published book.

On the day, we were delighted to be offered a lunch and a sublimely yummy dessert as part of my perks for giving the talk. After the meal everybody moved from the dining room to the function room for my presentation.

Randy and I had set up our screen here to show Randy's excellent still photos and video clips that illustrated my talk on Hidden Historic Gems of the Cotswolds. I interwove little known historic information with amusing anecdotes of my adventures as I gathered research for my book. Following this there was a Q & A. My talk was well received; I got laughs in all the right places and afterwards had interesting chats with readers as I signed my books for them.

In addition to droolingly delicious desserts, another of my perks was a gift – *The Great British Puddings Cook Book*. This gorgeous book is filled with recipes for mouth-watering desserts from different eras and now takes pride of place on my cookery book shelf.

From this event I was invited to open the Enstone Show and Fete. I was very pleased to accept, as Cotswold TV were to be on hand with their producer and director

Colin and Tom Wakefield to film an interview with me by their top broadcaster, the always prepared and model-beautiful Rowena Perkins. Rowena was one of the few interviewers who had actually read my book before the filming. Of course, there isn't always time for presenters to do this but when possible it makes for a much better interview.

Visitors to the Cotswolds would do well to look at the Cotswolds TV channel before and during their stay. It is imaginatively presented and an excellent resource for discovering what is currently going on in this area and has a wealth of background material too, that is interesting and useful.

I was particularly happy to open the Enstone Fete as this would also give me an opportunity to explore the area. I had wanted to do so since reading a special book that has become something of a classic. *Lifting the Latch* recounts the life of a modest farm worker, Montague Abbot (or 'Old Mont' as he was known), as told to the author Sheila Stewart.

This book is the story of his life, which encompasses nearly 80 years of working as a carter and shepherd in the tight-knit community of Enstone. His tale is particularly touching and, despite his impoverished circumstances and at times tragic destiny, Old Mont's sardonic humour, dignity and tenacity shine through. This book provides an extraordinarily vivid picture of life in those long ago times and I found I couldn't put it down. After finishing it I wanted to visit the Enstone of today to imagine what it would have been like to live there during Old Mont's time.

On the day of the fête we set off early to explore the area. As we travelled I mentioned to Randy that because I was opening this event it would mean that I would miss being able to do my usual Bric-a-Brac Dash.

This involved buying items from the bric-a-brac or white elephant stall that were featured at many of the summer fêtes. I had discovered that these were a great resource for furnishing our cottage at minimal cost.

Summer fêtes are a charming feature of Cotswold life, however their bucolic image is often shattered in the nitty gritty of the bargain hunt at their bric-a-brac stalls. Fantastic bargains are to be had at some of them but to win out it is best to arrive early and be ready to do battle. Action around the bric-a-brac stall often resembles a contact sport, with the combatants queuing up well ahead of the advertised opening time, quivering in anticipation like racehorses at the starting gate. The moment that the fête opens Olympic records are broken in the Bric-a-Brac Dash for the best bargain. Sharp elbows, large wicker baskets and foot stomping are the usual means of beating back the competition.

I developed a technique of having my husband stand in one place while I fling bargains at him to hang on to until I can pay. I am able then to whip around the stall at lightning speed. One of my rivals thought I was taking an unfair advantage and whacked the back of my husband's knees with her basket. He went down like a felled tree and narrowly escaped with his life as a surging mass of bargain hunters clambered over him, oblivious of his cries of pain.

My biggest prize was won when the vicar at the Church Westcote Fête announced, after the first surge of buying was over, that everything on the bric-a-brac stall was reduced to half price. I had been coveting an early 19th century tilt-top side table that all of us bargain hunters had considered too expensive. I was standing next to this table at the very moment that the vicar's words electrified the rabid crowd, so I instantly threw my body over the table yelling 'sold!'. This table was worth several hundred pounds and I braced myself as a heaving rugby scrum of humanity landed on top of me. I escaped suffocation only after the vicar bellowed for order through his megaphone. Somehow I still had possession of the table, which I bought for a few pounds, and it has pride of place beside the sofa in our cottage's living room. I think there is still an impression of my features in the French polish after being crushed face down by my bargain hunting rivals. It is all great fun and many treasured antiques, attractive knick-knacks and practical household necessities have been won from these gladiatorial bouts.

Before going to the fête I had read up on Enstone, as I wanted to be a little better informed about it before talking to the locals. I discovered that this collection of small villages in Oxfordshire, which is four miles east of Chipping Norton, acquired its name from a standing stone called the Ent Stone. This was part of a neolithic tomb, now a scheduled monument, near the Charlbury Road. It is thought to have some connection with the Rollright Stones, another neolithic site in Little Compton, not far from nearby Chipping Norton.

This massive rock is also known as the Hoar Stone and is actually situated closer to the hamlet of Fulwell. Once part of the Manor of Spelsbury, this small and charming hamlet's name is derived from the original 'foul well'.

The sleepy side-by-side ancient villages of Church Enstone and Neat Enstone, which are now simply grouped together as Enstone, appear not to have changed much since Old Mont's time, and though not quite chocolate-box pretty have a number of beautiful features and their own charm.

We passed several absolutely splendid, perfectly thatched cottages that were covered in roses before our first stop, St. Kenelm's Church in Church Enstone. This impressive building was first started in 850 A.D. and has gone through nine building phases. We admired the 14th century porch with its carved zig-zag stone mouldings and, inside, both agreed that the Enstone War Memorial window of pre-Raphaelite stained glass was fascinating. Its colours were muted, no bright reds and greens here, and the scenes portrayed were executed in intricate detail. It is thought to have been made by the William Morris Company, world-renowned for textile, wallpaper and household designs, and the quality of the craftsmanship certainly points to this being so.

In the south chapel is an amusing rustic tomb showing a strange, three dimensional figure, Stevens Wisdom, painted bright blue, kneeling before his own memorial telling him that he met his maker in 1633!

Randy photographed several of the very interesting gargoyles and grotesques on the outside of the church before we moved on to the nearby Crown Pub.

Apart from a 20th century extension off to the side, this charming pub's interior appears to have remained unchanged since it was built in the 17th century. Thankfully, it has not been 'trendied up' in any way and its slightly shabby look adds to its interest. We had a good comfort food pub lunch here before exploring the surrounding village. Finally, we stopped for a coffee at the local village shop in Neat Enstone called The Neat Retreat, which also includes a post office, tea room, grocery store and art gallery, before heading to the fête.

At the Enstone Fête opening, with the Cotswolds TV cameras whirring away, I felt as though I was following in the high-heeled shoes of the movie actress and champion country fête opener, Elizabeth Hurley. However, I managed not to get my stilettos stuck in the grass and do a face-plant, gave my speech and declared the fete well and truly open. There was a burst of applause as I plunged right into book signing.

When I mentioned to one of the locals how much I liked the book, *Lifting the Latch*, he told me of a guided tour coming up shortly entitled 'In Search of Old Mont' which showed visitors his haunts around Enstone that are mentioned in this book. Randy and I promised to return on the appointed day and take the tour.

After a few more weeks passed with no word about the planning permission being granted, Randy called Mr A but was told that planning committees take their sweet time and there is nothing to be done to hurry them.

I was beginning to have dreams of running out of money and walking around the streets in bare feet. Surely this couldn't go on much longer? I couldn't imagine what could be taking so long. Patience was advised by the Listed Property Owners' Club who agreed with the architect that nothing could be done.

Fortunately, a diversion presented itself when the day of the guided tour of Old Mont's haunts from *Lifting the Latch* had rolled around. Charlbury Station is close to

Enstone, so we stopped on the way as Randy wanted to take photos for the picture gallery on my web site.

I had written briefly of it in my earlier book, *Cotswolds Memoir*, and on this day this lovely little station, built in 1875 and tucked down a country lane, sparkled in the sun from a recent rain shower, and looked very smart in newly-painted, creamy heritage colours.

On the platform I was astonished to see a tabby cat sleeping on a woman's lap as she sat waiting for a train.

"How sweet. Do you always travel with your cat?" I asked.

It turned out that this was Stan the station cat who spent his days hanging round the ticket office, nuzzling passengers, climbing on their laps and purring contentedly until a train came along.

One of the friendly railway staff, who seemed tremendously proud of this charming Grade II listed station told me that a number of railway stations have acquired a cat. He mentioned that Huddersfield Station actually has a cat flap built into the ticket barrier and also that, incredibly, Tama a Japanese cat has been made station master of Idakiso station near Osaka, complete with his own tiny station-master cap. This had led to a 20 percent increase in business on the line.

As I listened, Stan had climbed onto my cat-whisperer husband Randy's lap and preened and purred with all the affection showered upon him. When he jumped down we followed him as he loped slowly along Platform 1, past Charlbury's Brunel-inspired wooden, Italianate chalet-style station building, and headed for the excellently maintained memorial garden at its end. This is dedicated to the late head of the railways, Sir Peter Parker, and features a lily pond complete with a dozen or so goldfish. Peter Parker lived near the station and was instrumental in helping save Chalbury from closure when cuts were made all over the country. Fortunately, the Cotswold Line Promotion Group continues his work by doing all in their power to ensure any further threats are warded off.

Stan hovered by the lily pond and stared hungrily at the darting fish. He made a few half-hearted swipes at them and then yawned and cleaned his face. Apparently, between trains Stan likes to lie in the change-well below the ticket window. When he fails to get out of the way in time, passengers sometimes have to retrieve their change from his fur. Stan has become something of a star around these parts as his picture is prominently displayed at the station and can be spotted through the ticket window. Chalbury Station looks for all the world like it belongs in one of those old Ealing comedies, or an episode of *Poirot,* and is well worth seeing whether or not a visitor is travelling by train. Apparently, having Stan hop on their lap and purr his way into their hearts has caused a number of cat-loving passengers to let the train to Paddington continue on without them.

By now rain clouds had formed overhead and after Randy bid a fond farewell to Stan we continued on to Enstone.

There were about fourteen of us who gathered, in search of Old Mont from *Lifting the Latch,* at St. Kenelm's Church in the now pouring rain to hike the four miles around several villages and hamlets, including those of Enstone (Church and Neat), Cleverley and the aforementioned Fulwell.

The walk was organised by Cotswold Volunteer Wardens. Tony our guide cheerfully rounded us up and we set off for a wonderful ramble across fields, through root-bound woodland, slipping and sliding over a number of stiles. Tony was a font of countryside knowledge, pointing out one narrow lane called Cling Clang, so named after the noise at dawn made by the cans of the milkman as he hurried along his route. We all shuddered as, next, he told us of another lane near Chipping Norton named in earlier times Swing Swang, the location of a hangman's gibbet.

We stopped every now and then for Tony to point out the various cottages Old Mont had inhabited in both Church and Neat Enstone. The walking group were a very friendly bunch and the rain didn't seem to matter at all as everybody chatted and got to know each other a little.

We stopped again when we reached Lennox Farm, where Old Mont worked taking his first job as a cowman at thirteen years of age. As he was experienced in handling horses he received a promotion to carter by the age of fifteen. We were interested to learn from Christine, a lively, knowledgeable member of the hiking group and former resident of Enstone, that it was here at Lennox Farm that her grandfather had taught Old Mont to milk cows. She had brought *Lifting the Latch* with her, and to everyone's enjoyment read to the group the passage in which her grandfather was described.

Further on, we were all amused when Tony pointed out the name of one of the cottages in which Old Mont had lived. This building belonged to the squire of Ditchley, and when Old Mont moved there to work on the estate he declared to the squire's agent who welcomed him into the cottage.

'Living 'ere I'll be as warm as a biddy's bottom.' He was referring to a hen's rear end warming eggs in the nest. Subsequently, this cottage was called Biddy's Bottom and is so named to this day.

This guided walk was so enjoyable I planned to look for more with Cotswold Volunteer Wardens. I discovered that the *Cotswold Lion Newspaper*, which lists these walks, can be found on the AONB web site and is available for a small subscription.

This little adventure brought Old Mont's world startlingly alive, so much so that there was a distinct feeling of stepping through a time warp as the landscape and cottages remain unchanged since his time there. This called for a re-read of *Lifting the Latch*, which would, I was sure, be even more rewarding as I had now seen so many of the locations mentioned in the book. I highly recommend this eloquent homage to the heroism of those who work on the land.

After this enjoyable outing we came back to earth to deal with our extension. We made a strict accounting of finances and tried to figure out where we stood, as I was getting more and more anxious about our situation. Almost four months had dragged by since our first failed application and the submission of the second one. There was still no word from the architect on whether our application had been granted. After a meticulous accounting and an attempt to project our costs over the next year, including all the building expenses, we were alarmed to find that our coffers were definitely inadequate. This, despite the recent injection of cash from my work in Hollywood and Randy's cartoon series.

I couldn't say I hadn't been warned, having heard many cautionary tales about cottage renovations turning into money pits. Why didn't I listen? Had the romantic dream of living in a cottage overcome all my common sense? Another horrible thought occurred to me. Even if we got planning permission, a further crisis could be looming on the horizon. If the building work was seriously delayed, and projects like this sometimes are, then this might mean that the cottage extension would not be finished in time for the filming to begin. In that case I would have to pay back the money I had borrowed against the contract. All this together with the fact that the seemingly endless waiting for planning permission was a big drain on our finances made me have a bad headache. We hadn't broken ground and not one stone was in place. I was truly in despair. I turned to Randy and whispered something I never thought I would say.

"Do you think we should give up on the extension and sell the cottage?"

Seven

TEA IN THE BALLROOM
Northleach, Yanworth, Winchcombe

Whoosh!

A great cloud of dust flew up as part of one of the cart shed walls began to crumble away. Two builders were making an opening for a window and saving as much of the Cotswold stone as possible. Another builder was working on the wall of the cottage and still another on the small piggery that would become the study/office/recording studio. Eventually these would be joined together to make these three buildings into the perfect cottage of my imagination. This would give us the space we needed to live and work. Randy and I hugged each other in relief. Hurray! Work had finally started on the extension.

Earlier, after much agonising, we had called the real estate agent to get an estimate of the cottage's current market value, with a view to selling it.

On that very day, Mr A had called. Our planning permission had finally been granted and we were free to build. We congratulated Mr A and got in touch with the Listed Property Owners' Club to relay the good news and thank them.

Mr A felt that it was extremely unlikely that the building work would overrun to the extent that it would interfere with the filming – so we decided to go ahead.

I was overjoyed – the thought of selling had plunged me into gloom but I knew that the risk of bankruptcy if we had to pay back the film loan would make me even gloomier. When Mr A had given us an estimate from his quantum surveyor we had put the work out to tender, making sure that the various companies we approached knew about this estimate. We finally decided on a team of local builders who had done other work nearby. We also engaged the services of Fred, a project manager who had been highly recommended.

Before the building began Randy moved his recording set-up out of the living room and into a caravan we had rented, which was now in the garden. The kitchen in our cottage was not being renovated, except for the floor, but as it was very close to the new building work, most of the utilities and the water were disconnected. It was not in a usable condition. Instead, we used the tiny kitchen in the caravan for cooking. Despite its size I was determined to cook as much as I could for the builders. I had read about a home owner who had cooked at least one tasty meal a week for his builders during a renovation and he felt that the goodwill it engendered had played a big part in the success and speedy finish of the work. I was determined to do the same thing, despite the limitations of the caravan.

Our poor garden was looking the worse for wear now that the caravan and the builders were in it. At one end a dry stone wall that had been a bit shaky and needed some work now started to cave in along one section.

I had always wanted to learn how to build a dry stone wall and as we needed to save every penny I thought I would investigate if it were possible for me to learn enough to repair it. Although I had observed a dry stone wall being built before, I wanted to take another look in more detail and this led me to Northleach and the rural life collection which is housed in the Old Prison.

A couple of days later, I left Randy working alongside the builders and took off with my friend Maria. I met her through writing my last book, *Cotswolds Memoir*, when she contacted me. She had enjoyed my book and offered to show me her off-the-beaten track discoveries in the Cotswolds. Her knowledge of Cotswold history and architecture was incredibly extensive and what she showed me was a revelation. We wrote to each other, initially, and became pen pals and now have one of those lasting friendships that I speak of in my introduction, which is a wonderful, unexpected perk of writing a book.

We made first for the Cotswolds Dry Stone Walling Academy, which is housed in the Grade II listed Old

Prison, on the Fosse Way in Northleach, Gloucestershire. This is now also the visitor attraction Escape to the Cotswolds and home to the Lloyd-Baker Rural Life collection. We strolled around, viewing the interesting collection of farm wagons, carts and farm implements and then toured the remarkably spacious prison cells which, I noticed, actually looked bigger than my first apartment. Apparently this was a model prison when it was built in the 1790s.

Outside in the grounds of the prison there was a whole array of rural skills being demonstrated, including sheep shearing, wool spinning and numerous others.

Everybody was chatting about the recent tour of the Old Prison by the Prince of Wales after having been invited by The Friends of the Cotswolds and the Cotswold Conservation Board, whose offices are also in this building. Apparently, the Prince was particularly interested in the rural skills on display and stopped to talk to the various artisans for quite some time.

As we watched the rural skills being demonstrated, it was fascinating to see a section of roof being thatched in exactly the way it has been done for centuries. Also, there was a blacksmith heating up wrought iron over a coke-fired brazier and hammering loudly to sculpt a lovely shape to be used in an estate fence. Finally, there was the dry stone walling demonstration and I was able to see again, in more detail, how it was done.

"It takes a fair bit of practice to get it right," said the builder, who was hefting stones up to the wall in a wheelbarrow when I inquired about picking up the technique. Watching him in action made me realise that it would be too big an undertaking right then to learn enough to repair the wall in our garden. But maybe one day I would have the time to take classes. There is information on dry stone walling courses are at the end of this narrative.

Maria and I then made our way to a less energetic activity – having delicious cakes and tea and settling in for a good gossip at the Lion Café which is also housed in the spacious Old Prison.

During our chat we had a chuckle at an item from a newspaper lying around in the café. I was drawn to the photo of a woman with an amazingly awful hairdo. Great lumpy white chunks of something or other were entwined in a mangled fashion in her hair. She did not look happy. It turned out that this woman was experiencing a bad hair day to end all bad hair days. Apparently she had mistaken (don't ask how) a can of hair mousse for another can containing expanding builder's foam, resulting in a rock hard helmet of cavity filler. This would be another DIY disaster story to add to our collection.

Next, we strolled the hundred yards or so to reach the centre of Northleach, as I had never explored this pretty town, which features a Gothic Revival Church, antique shops and small boutiques. The town also has three pubs and we had time to look over one of them, the Wheatsheaf, which has been tastefully remodelled and, I noted for a future visit, had a lovely garden. This would make the perfect setting for a pub lunch. Best of all, Northleach had a butcher and a baker.

On the way back I described to Maria a visit Randy and I had made to nearby Yanworth, near Northleach. It was to tour Stowell Park Garden, one of the most glorious gardens I have ever seen.

I am always trying to peek over the walls of lovely gardens in the Cotswolds, especially those belonging to the large estates. Now I have discovered that I can actually see the fabulous gardens of many of the manor house estates by tracking down their open days on the National Garden Scheme Open Garden Days. And Stowell Park was one of them. A few weeks earlier, Randy and I had spent a wonderful afternoon visiting the magnificent grounds of Lord and Lady Vestey, which features arguably the best private garden in the country. Stowell House crowns a hill commanding matchless views across the unspoiled Gloucestershire countryside. One elegant terrace after another, carpeted in velvet lawn, unfolds down the slopes below the house, eventually merging seamlessly into the rolling hills of the Coln Valley.

A parade of pleached limes frame the approach to the 14th century manor house and give way to a long rose pergola and wide, plant-filled borders containing a fine collection of roses.

As we approached the gardens we were amused to see a small sign which read 'Teas in the Ballroom'. Somehow this conjured up an image from old movies of thé dansant (an afternoon tea dance) in the 1930s with perhaps Noel Coward as a guest and Ambrose's orchestra playing a peppy foxtrot. Tea could either be taken in the vast, wood-panelled ballroom or on one of the sunny terraces with that gorgeous view below.

By having tea in the ballroom it was possible to see a little of the inside of this historic manor house, always my ambition, and is sometimes a wonderful bonus with the NGS Open Garden Days.

Stowell House garden covers eight acres and also features, among other attractions, three peach houses, an acre of fruit and vegetables laid out in two walled gardens and a woodland walk.

Lady Vestey and her head gardener, Neil Hewertson, have created a true gem at Stowell Park, making this a must-see garden. This NGS Open Garden event was hosted by the Cobalt Charity Trust and we were happy to make a donation.

Many of the gardens on these private estates are open only one or two days a year, so it is a good idea to do some advanced planning. It is a great way to explore the Cotswolds. We got hold of a National Garden Scheme book that tells of every open garden for the year. It is as thick as a novel but is invaluable to have in the car. Whenever there was some spare time between explorations or appointments we would flip through the book to see if an NGS Open Garden was nearby. All information on the gardens is also online: details at the end of this narrative.

Afterwards, we took a quick tour of the small rural parish of Yanworth, part of the Stowell Park Estate, including St. Michael's Church which originated around the year 1200 and is set somewhat apart from the village.

A look at the local village, a trek around a couple of gorgeous estate gardens followed by the occasional peek inside a manor house and finally having tea with a bun is my idea of a perfect Cotswold outing.

I promised Maria that I would accompany her on a visit to Stowell Park Garden the very next time there was an open day.

Returning from Northleach, we pulled up in front of the cottage as clouds of dust drifted out onto the lane. It was wonderful to see all the activity. It continued at the same pace over the next few weeks as the builders framed in the new bathroom and worked on the cart shed. They were leaving the piggery until last as there was discussion about whether the roof joists were too far gone and the roof would have to be replaced.

The repointing that Randy was doing seemed endless so our kind friends rallied again for a repointing party on a Sunday when the builders were not around. I joined in with Sandra, Jim, Susan, Bob, Ed and Carol. We worked until it was time to serve dinner. Susan had offered her kitchen to me, so earlier that day we worked together to prepare the evening's meal. It was so lovely to cook in a proper kitchen again and I enjoyed making super delicious Cornish pasties. These would be easy to heat up and eat without having to deal with knives and forks. I asked the butcher to make mince, or ground beef as they call it in America, from a good cut of steak and then instead of potatoes added par boiled parsnips. I dried these out after the par boiling and fried them in a little butter and garlic before putting them in with all the other ingredients. These included mushrooms, shallots, garlic, lots of spices and finally a little curry powder, which made the pasties really tasty. I wrapped each pasty in tin foil so that they could be re-heated easily in the caravan stove top and oven.

Susan made a pot of split pea soup and poured this into several soup Thermos flasks to be served in mugs. For dessert she made a treacle tart that was served on paper serviettes.

After dinner I poured some delicious sloe gin for everybody that Randy and I had made the previous year from the sloes we had picked from among the hedgerows around our village.

As we sipped our drinks the conversation drifted into describing amusing dreams. Carol recounted a dream that involved Donald Trump's hair.

In her dream, Donald Trump, the American property tycoon known for his unbelievably complex comb-over, was standing on a London street on an extremely windy day. There was a sudden tremendous whoosh of wind that lifted this comb-over up at right angles to his head. When this happened it appeared to be of such an incredible height that it was now taller than the building Trump was standing next to, which happened to be The Shard.

This led us on to telling stories of various toupée fails.

Our actor friend Bob remembered his father telling him about an incident years ago when Charlton Heston, the star of *Ben Hur*, was playing the lead in *A Man for all Seasons* in a West End theatre in London.

Apparently, Heston made a terrific movie star but his stage acting left a lot to be desired and the fact that he had the gall to go up against all the excellent English actors was ill-advised.

Heston wore a toupée and, despite the fact that this was apparent even to Martians from outer space, he pretended to everyone that his hair was real. He even tried to fool his dresser at the theatre, which meant he had to wear a wig for his character in *A Man for all Seasons* on top of his own toupée! This was so ridiculous and his acting so bad that a leading London newspaper's reviewer declined to write about the play and, instead, simply reviewed Charlton Heston's two wigs. It was not a rave review.

Next, I chimed in remembering a fake hair encounter from my volleyball playing days. This took place on the beach in Los Angeles with a bunch of actor friends. One of them, who I shall call Nigel, had a toupée that he thought passed for real hair, however, it was so obviously fake that is could have been easily spotted as such from the Canadian border.

His wife inadvertently confirmed what everybody knew by making way too many references to Nigel's 'hair growing so fast he's always having to get it cut' and Nigel 'inheriting his thick head of hair from his father's side of the family' and so on.

During a break from volleyball one day, Nigel, the wig wearing wonder, offered to teach me a little bit about surfing. So together with his wife and a crowd of the players we waded into the sea. As Nigel was showing me how to climb on a surf board a particularly high wave swept over his head. Taken by surprise he emerged from the wave spluttering water and as bald as a coot. His wife, pointing at his chrome dome glinting in the sun, screamed, "Nigel – your piece!" Horrified, he clapped both hands to his bald head and exclaimed, "But they said I could swim in it!"

His wife, now abandoning all pretence, shouted in panic, "That piece cost three thousand dollars. Quick everybody, help find it!" The volleyball crowd happily spent the next hour toupée-diving in the surf. Sadly, the toupee was never found despite many of the wags among these players frequently fetching up huge clumps of wiggling, stinky seaweed and yelling, "Is this it?"

Susan, who is an actress and comedy writer, laughed a lot at this and said, "I have always wanted to write a book called 'The Toupee Spotter's Handbook' that would give tips and instructions on finding the fakes."

Ed replied, "So you're are an expert, are you?"

"Yes, I think so," said Susan, "I think bald is beautiful and the pretence of a piece is insane. Everybody knows, so what is the point. I can spot one a mile off."

"Really, I hope you haven't spotted any around here," said Ed, glancing round at the other men in the room.

"Of course not," said Susan, "thankfully no one has one here or I'd be really red-faced."

With that Ed took hold of his hair and ripped it off his head.

We all collapsed with laughter as Ed stood there, totally bald, with a huge grin on his face and a neat piece of toupée tape stuck above each ear.

As Ed waved his toupée at Susan, she covered her red face with her hands and groaned. It made for a hilarious end to the evening.

The next day, Randy and I took off in a battered old pickup truck we had rented for collecting building materials and made for the reclamation yard in Winchcombe. Randy wanted to look for more flagstones for the piggery and to buy some timber for fencing. This yard is almost hidden up a narrow lane near a petrol station just outside Winchcombe. While there were stacks of timber and other building materials which Randy was happy to see, I didn't feel this was as interesting as the Cotswolds Reclamation Yard. There was no statuary or antiques. However, it did give me the opportunity of turning our visit into a whistle-stop tour of this area, beginning with a stop at Winchcombe as I wanted to explore this picturesque, ancient village.

There are many interesting buildings here, some of them half-timbered Tudor and others 17th century, all packed in together, higgledy-piggledy, perching it appears somewhat precariously on the hilly terrain. The high street is crowded with small shops and even has a hardware store, a must-see for Randy. We rooted around in it for a while until he found some tools he needed, then headed for the Tourist Information Centre. Here I discovered that Winchcombe is a nexus for hikers as it sits on six long-distance footpaths: The Cotswold, Gloucestershire, Wychavon, Windrush and St. Kenelm's Way and the St. Kenelm's Trail. A walking festival is held in Winchcombe every May.

We took lots of snaps of the camera-ready streets but could not resist the temptation to take a break when we came across The Lady Grey Tearoom, housed in a lovely ancient building with an elegant interior and more tables for fine weather scattered around a small, pretty garden at the back. Served among many other delicacies were: Tarte Citron, Welsh and poacher's rarebit, classic afternoon tea with scones and clotted cream, home-made ice-cream and an array of delicious pastries baked on the premises. I chose a fragrant almond slice that had come straight out of the oven and Randy had an enormous doorstep of lemon cake that was as light as a feather. Our sugar rush gave us the energy needed to zip further along the street on the way to explore St. Peter's Church.

It was built between 1452 and 1462 from the wealth of medieval wool merchants, and bills itself at the Parish Church of the ancient capital of Mercia. There has been a church on this site since the 9th century and St. Peter's is famous for its amusing and whimsical grotesque stone carvings that decorate the outside of the building. Randy got busy setting up his telephoto camera lens on a tripod, as many of these carvings are high up or on battlements and the roof of the church. Often erroneously described as gargoyles these carvings are more properly known as grotesques as none of them have the defining gargoyle characteristic – the ability to carry away excess water from the church roof through a down spout integrated into its carving.

We laughed out loud at the hilarious expressions of the grotesques and vied with each other to point out the funniest one. We had plenty to choose from as there are 40 carvings around the outside of the church. Twenty of them are of grimacing, demonic creatures and the remainder are caricatures of important local figures. Perhaps the most famous of the grotesques, due to its frequent appearance on postcards of the Cotswolds, is that of a carving on the east of the porch. This human figure, wearing a squared-off pudding basin hat, has an especially idiotic expression featuring a lop-sided mouth, round poppy eyes and a long horse-like face. This carving is thought to be the model for the Mad Hatter in Lewis Carroll's *Alice in Wonderland*.

The grotesques would be enough reason to visit but this church has it all going on: altar vestments stitched by Catherine of Aragon, coffins of King Kenwulph and his son St. Kenelm from an earlier Saxon church on the same site, a 16th century parish chest, floor tiles and a door from Winchcombe Abbey, Civil War bullet holes and an impressive 90-foot high West Tower. In addition, this church is unique in that it is a complete rebuild, accomplished in the astonishingly short time of ten years, therefore its English Gothic, Perpendicular architecture is completely uniform in style.

Visitors should take a good look, too, at the 15th century medieval rood screen situated at the west end of the nave. Almost hidden in its exquisitely carved intricate scrollwork and fanciful foliage, featuring vines and lizards, is a small face, which has been inserted by the wood carver and has become known as the Winchcombe Imp. It is fun to resist having it pointed out and to spot it unaided.

Just west of the south porch we spotted the grinning face of Sir Ralph Boteler of Sudeley, who contributed money to complete the church.

This led us on to explore Sudeley Castle, after I persuaded Randy that we couldn't miss it as it was so close.

Arriving at Sudeley Castle the drama of its barbaric history was obvious at first glance.

First built in the 10th century it is mentioned in the Domesday Book and its numerous owners have contributed to its rich and exciting story. Ethelred the Unready, who maintained a deer park among the oak trees in the grounds, King Richard III, who died at the Battle of Bosworth, and Ethelred's sister, Goda, a relative of William of Normandy, are just a few of the notable names who feature in its history.

Sudeley was spared during the Norman invasion and eventually the castle was acquired by Ralph Boteler, an admiral in the French wars who used his wealth to rebuild it in 1442.

Seized in a forced sale by Edward IV in 1469, the castle, after going through several more owners, was subsequently granted to the 1st Baron Thomas Seymour. It was visited by Henry VIII and his second wife Anne Boleyn, and here its history begins to resemble a soap opera plot as Baron Seymour eventually married the current King's stepmother, Henry VIII's sixth wife, Catherine Parr.

Other famous names associated with Sudeley include Lady Jane Grey, a ward of Baron Seymour's and Lady

Elizabeth Tudor – later Queen Elizabeth I, daughter of Henry VIII.

Those Tudors certainly knew how to throw a party, for in 1592 the castle was the scene of a week-long festivity attended by Queen Elizabeth I, to celebrate the anniversary of the defeat of the Spanish Armada. Baron Seymour built up Sudeley into a magnificent palace for his new wife Catherine Parr, but after only two years of marriage she died tragically giving birth to their daughter, Mary. She was buried in St. Mary's chapel in the grounds of the castle.

As we walked through the grounds we noted a visually dramatic ruined section of the castle, its vast, roofless walls giving an indication of the castle's massive size at this time. This part of the castle, along with the chapel, had been desecrated by Cromwell's men when they stormed it, commandeering it as their garrison headquarters. The entire estate was plundered, ransacked and left an abandoned ruin.

Today the castle is a splendid place to visit, with a tour that includes 20 treasures of Sudeley. On display are a collection of unique artefacts and works of art of great historical importance, which we found fascinating. Sudeley also hosts regular events, including talks from historians, children's days, seasonal events, family fun days, jazz performances, picnics and book signings.

Gardens are a big favourite of mine and the sunny day made it a joy to stroll around the glorious gardens that surround the castle. There are nine different gorgeous, garden 'rooms', the centrepiece being the Queen's Garden featuring hundreds of varieties of roses. The Knot Garden was inspired by a dress pattern worn by Elizabeth I that hangs in the castle and we took numerous photographs of the box hedges, over a thousand in number, that form its intricate, geometric design.

I was imagining how lovely it would be to stay in this gorgeous place when I discovered that it is actually possible to do so. Accommodation can be booked in the Sudeley Castle Country Cottages situated at the edge of the estate. Eleven Cotswolds stone cottages surround a charming central courtyard and are set in landscaped gardens. Perhaps the reason that Sudeley seems so lively and interesting today is because it is one of the few castles in Britain that is still a residence.

Lady Ashcombe has lived in Sudeley for over 40 years and owns the castle along with her children Mollie and Mark Dent-Brocklehurst. Lady Ashcombe has overcome great difficulties to bring the castle back to its present glory. When she was widowed the family were weighed down with responsibilities and a decision was made to have major renovations completed and to open the castle as a visitor attraction. What a brilliant decision it was – leading to the success that Sudeley Castle is today. Everything about this lovely venue gets full marks from me and I hope visitors to the Cotswolds enjoy touring it as much as I did.

As we arrived back from our visit to Winchcombe it was obvious that a crisis was going on. The builders were all grouped around the piggery and looking at it apprehensively. The roof had just been carefully taken off but this had made the walls more unstable than anticipated and the whole building was in danger of tumbling down at any moment. This would be a disaster as we knew we wouldn't get planning permission to rebuild it from scratch. If it fell down it would mean no study and nowhere to work. As we all stood looking at the piggery, one of its walls sagged a tiny bit outwards and a stone teetered and then tumbled ominously from its top.

Eight

SAVING THE PIGGERY
Faringdon, Stanton Harcourt, Standlake

"Look out! There go more stones... quick, help me unload the fence posts!"

My hand trembled as I put the kettle on. I couldn't look any more. If the walls of the piggery were going to fall I didn't want to watch.

I vividly remembered Mrs Murgatroyd describing her renovation of Stable Cottage, one of the holiday lets we had rented from her. Part of the roof had been taken off when she heard a shout and saw four builders suddenly running for their lives. She couldn't understand why they were bolting until a second later, with a loud rumble, an entire wall fell down.

Outside, I could hear Randy and the builders leaping into action. Fred, the project manager, wasn't there that day so Randy directed the builders as they all worked quickly to prop up the walls. Willing the walls to stay up, I made tea for everyone with my heart in my mouth. Luckily, at the reclamation yard in Winchcombe, Randy had bought timber for fencing and fence posts for enclosing part of our land that was not bordered by dry stone walls. He quickly got the builders to help unload these and used them to prop up the walls. Next there were furious amounts of banging and sawing as some crudely made buttresses, rather like the flying buttresses used on churches, were fashioned for a more permanent solution to the problem. Sweat poured off Randy and the builders as they raced against time to get the walls stable. When the last brace was propped in place and the piggery was still standing a big cheer went up. My hands continued to shake as I had a little blub into my tea with relief.

Building an extension for a listed building, as I was finding out, is not for the faint-hearted. Now a new roof had to be built on the piggery. Apparently this was not an easy matter so we didn't have the all clear yet.

The drama with the piggery had actually had the surprising effect of bonding us with the builders, softening their manner a little. Randy's leadership and quick action had certainly saved the day and it was clear to them now that he wasn't just some Yankee toff, but had some building experience himself. My weekly meal for the builders was about due so to show my gratitude I went all out to cook a really tasty dish for them.

I put together Pot au Feu, which translates to Pot over the Fire and is basically chicken soup. Thrifty French cooks would, in past times, keep a pot of soup going continuously over an open fire or the cooking range and throw in every unused scrap of food from other dishes, in order not to waste a morsel. I threw in everything I had in the larder and what I had growing in the garden for my version of this classic dish.

I used boneless chicken thighs, together with chicken stock and barley. A neighbour had brought over some courgettes from her allotment to which I added onions, shallots, celery, Portobello mushrooms and red peppers. I used a big chunk of fresh ginger and chopped it up along with a whole head of garlic. I sautéed the onions, shallots, garlic and ginger first and then the chicken before adding the chicken stock and a big slosh of white wine. I flavoured the soup with lots of herbs and creole spices, then added a glug of tamari, which is sort of like Bovril but made from soy. From our garden I added Moroccan mint, fresh chives and thyme, along with some chard I had growing in a pot. I simmered my Pot au Feu for ages and then thickened it with a little kuzu as it cooked. I roasted sweet potatoes in the caravan oven and chopped them into small chunks, placing these in the bottom of soup bowls and ladling chicken and soup on top. The sweet potatoes were mashed up at the bottom of the soup bowl where they soaked up the rich, tasty liquid, already thickened from the barley and kuzu, making the whole dish chunky and hearty. The sweet potatoes blended perfectly with the garlic infused onions and the complexity of all the spices. It tasted delicious – even if I do say so myself. To finish off, I found some cheddar cheese and grated that on top, thickening up the Pot au Feu even more. This meal seemed to go over very well with the builders. There was enough left over for Randy and I to make another meal from it so I stowed this in the fridge in the caravan for the next day.

I wouldn't have time to cook the following day as I had been invited to participate in Heritage Day in Faringdon. I was to do a book signing, sell my books and give a series of short talks on the history of the Cotswolds throughout the day.

English Heritage regularly open all of their historic buildings to the public in various towns and this event in Faringdon was teamed with a number of other fun activities so the town was going to be 'en-fête'. My perch was to be in the Pump House, a beautiful listed building in the market square.

Randy and I had visited Faringdon a couple of months earlier and enjoyed touring this small town, which bills itself 'The Threshold of the Cotswolds' as it is on the very edge of this lovely area. While Faringdon does not possess some of the glamour of the picture-perfect Cotswolds villages, it has many interesting features, including, on this particular day, a bustling market in the town square. This market has been a feature of Faringdon since King Henry II gave the town a Royal Charter in 1218. Faringdon is also untouched by too much commercial exploitation and full of very friendly people.

On that day we wandered into the Tourist Information Office and met one of them, Beth the manager. After chatting for a while she not only offered to stock my book *Cotswolds Memoir* in the Tourist Office but then invited me, as a local author, to do a book signing for the upcoming Heritage Day that would sing the praises of Faringdon. She then handed us a map featuring all the highlights of the town.

We strolled over to explore the first highlight, All Saints' Church, which originated in the 13th century. It looks rather odd as it is missing its steeple, thought to have been lopped off by a few cannon balls during the civil war but is still very interesting. There is a splendid collection of monuments in the church and a Norman nave.

A short walk from the marketplace is Faringdon's Folly Tower and Woodland. The folly was built in 1935 by music composer Lord Berners, who lived in nearby Faringdon House from 1918 until 1950.

The helpful staff at the Tourist Information Office had shown us how to catch an over-the-wall glimpse of Faringdon House, which we planned to do once we got back to our car.

The eccentric Lord Berners was known for his collection of pet fantail doves which he dyed pink, in addition to a variety of other colours, and released to fly all over the town. On the days that it is open to the public a climb to the top of the Folly features gorgeous views over five counties.

On sale in the Tourist Information Office is a copy of *The Mad Boy, Lord Berners, My Grandmother and Me* by Sofka Zinovieff, a local author who inherited Faringdon House. This entertaining and well-written book gives an account of the bohemian and eccentric goings on in this house during the long ago era of Lord Berner's tenure. He entertained all the luminaries of the day, including several of the Mitford sisters and one of my favourite authors, Evelyn Waugh.

To digress a little, I was fascinated to find that the inspiration for Evelyn Waugh's book, *Brideshead Revisited*, was Madresfield House in the Malvern Hills and not, as is often thought, Castle Howard. This common misconception probably came about because the televised adaptation of *Brideshead Revisited* used Castle Howard in Yorkshire for its film location.

Evelyn Waugh was at Oxford with Hugh Lygon, whose aristocratic family owned Madresfield House. He was invited back to stay by his friend during university vacations and based some of his book on his experiences there. I was interested to read *Madresfield: One House. One Family. One Thousand Years* by Jane Mulvagh, which describes this house and its history and Evelyn Waugh's involvement with the whole family. At this point in time Madresfield was occupied by the 7th Earl of Beauchamp (Hugh's father), his wife and seven children.

Even though Madresfield House is not in the Cotswolds – it is only an hour's drive north and is well worth a visit, we had to make an appointment to see it and managed to squeeze in with a small tour that was already scheduled. I found it absolutely fascinating to spot various features of the house, like the small chapel attached, that had inspired passages in *Brideshead Revisited.*

Back in Faringdon we also enjoyed discovering its collection of independent stores, among them a gift shop, a coffee shop that serves Lebanese food and an excellent haute cuisine deli, The Hare in the Woods. We chatted to the owner, Lesley, who had us taste some of her delicious home-made offerings, including a wonderful pastry flan of beetroot, cheese and red peppers. She also offered a jumbo-sized sausage roll, made with pork mixed with her own special herb concoction and enveloped in thin delicate pastry. We left, loaded down with packages of Lesley's smoked mackerel, lamb tagine and chicken curry and a promise by her, as she caters too, to make a cake for Randy, decorated with the stars and stripes of the American flag. He likes to celebrate Independence Day and a glorious cake was made by her for the 4th of July that was the hit of a barbeque we hosted to mark the occasion.

As I arrived on Heritage Day lots of visitors were already pouring into Faringdon, making for a wonderful turn out as the Town Cryer clanged his bell and strode through the town announcing all the day's activities.

I set up my book signing table on my assigned slot on the second floor of the Pump House in the same room with three or four other presenters, displaying fossils found near Faringdon and masses of old postcards that showed views of the town from the last century. Crowds of people interested in historic buildings came through and I had lovely chats with many of them who stopped by on their tour of the Pump House.

It was a wonderful day as I managed to tour the Heritage open houses, sold a pile of books which added some more money to the cottage extension coffers and discussed the history of the area with some really interesting people.

Heritage Day ended early enough for my pen pal Maria to take me on a little jaunt afterwards. When I had mentioned my 'Hidden Gems of the Cotswolds' talk to her she suggested showing me some new treasures to add to it.

We shared an absolute passion for the Cotswolds and for historic buildings in this region in particular. We couldn't get enough of discovering new ones together and discussing the merits of the various architectural styles.

My keen interest in art, architecture and historic houses had been fostered by my mother and I was very grateful to her for doing so.

She tried very hard to give her children a cultural education. This was no easy task as she had come from a very impoverished childhood. Luckily, teachers at her school had spotted her above-average intelligence and picked her out as their best bet to be the first student to win a scholarship to go on to grammar school. This was something never before achieved by a student at her primary school. After a lot of hard work, she passed, got to grammar school and received an excellent education for a working class child. However, despite her ambition to be an educated and refined lady, her bawdy Cockney beginnings often had a way of re-surfacing, much to our delight. Nonetheless, she was determined to elevate her children and one day decided, as we were at that time in our early teens, that we were old enough to appreciate dance. She found a ballet programme on television and rounded us all up to watch.

We all squashed together with the cat on our bumpy sofa, in front of a roaring fire, to watch *Swan Lake* or perhaps it was *Sleeping Beauty*, with the serious intention of absorbing some culture.

Before the programme began, my mother had hauled in a mountain of food for us all to eat during the viewing. She acted as if we would all suffer from malnutrition if we had to get through even a television show without enough snacks to feed a small army. She insisted on piling on the food, despite the fact that she had, within the last hour, served us a delicious three-course meal.

So, true to form she stacked up a raft of snacks – always the same: at least a half dozen jumbo-sized bars of fruit and nut chocolate that seemed to be as thick as a telephone book. So thick, in fact, that we had to hammer these huge slabs with the fire poker to break them into pieces small enough to eat. There were masses of bags of potato crisps of every flavour and as if that wasn't enough there would be a least a dozen oranges. These my mother would peel throughout the viewing. All this was washed down with gallons of fizzy lemonade which made us fit to burst.

We would solemnly watch as the ballet began. After a few minutes, however, when some male, muscle-bound ballet dancers leaped across the screen, Mum just couldn't help herself.

"Oh that one's not shy about showing off his meat and two veg," she wailed.

"Oh Mum, look at that one. Did he forget to put his trousers on?" I asked, pointing at the screen.

As if on cue, the camera seemed to zoom in on the uh... em... area in question.

Mum squealed, "Oh no, not a close up! I don't know how they allow this stuff on TV. You can see his entire three-piece suite!"

"Look Mum," I exclaimed, "all the blokes are getting ready to dance on together for the big finish!"

By now all of us would be hysterical with laughter, tears pouring down our cheeks as we doubled over on the sofa, scaring the cat, crushing the hill of potato crisp bags and sending the oranges rolling across the room. Just when we felt we would faint from the pain in our sides the final line up of husky ballet dancers filled the screen.

"Oh no," gasped my mother, "not all of them on together, Saints preserve us, it's enough to put your eye out!"

Despite the laughter the dances provoked, my mother's efforts to elevate us yielded the desired results as I gradually acquired a passion for history, historic houses and architecture, which has not only given me endless pleasure but is the basis of my work as an author. However, try as I might, ballet is the one discipline I find difficult to take seriously.

Maria's little jaunt involved taking me to see an enclave of historic houses at Stanton Harcourt in Oxfordshire, a few miles from Witney. This village's name means 'Farmhouse by the Stones', which no doubt refers to the nearby prehistoric stone circle, the Devil's Quoits, a smaller version of Stone Henge, just southwest of the village and also well worth a visit.

The quiet Oxfordshire village of Stanton Harcourt features a number of treasures. It was visited by the production team of the television show *Time Team* and, during the dig, Palaeolithic bones, teeth and tusks were found. However, Maria wanted to show me the Grade II listed Harcourt House, built for the Harcourt family in the 15th and mid-16th centuries, and in a separate building its Great Kitchen, built in 1485.

The service range attached to the south of the Great Kitchen is also 15th century and has since been converted. It is now Manor Farmhouse.

I was transfixed by the beauty of this collection of unspoiled historic buildings but there was more to come. Maria then took me to see Pope's Tower, in the grounds of Harcourt House, which was built 1470. The tower did not acquire its name until the poet Alexander Pope stayed there in 1717 and used its upper room to translate a part of Homer's *Iliad*.

This village, thankfully devoid of visitors, has a very special atmosphere. It seems remote and somehow even mysterious. As we walked around, noticing the many thatched ancient cottages, and admiring, now from a distance, the group of Harcourt medieval buildings, it truly felt as if we had stepped back in time.

Next, we visited Standlake, a mile or so away, and were fascinated to see more lovely old buildings, notably Standlake Manor a Grade II listed half-timbered Tudor house on this village's main street. This was particularly special as the timbering was much more prevalent and closely spaced than was usual. The surfeit of timbering apparently denoted the prosperity of the original owner.

This village is close to where the Windrush River meets the Thames and Palaeolithic finds have been discovered here also.

There are two pubs in Standlake, The Black Horse and the Bell. Maria and I decided that we would come back to the Bell, with our husbands, on another occasion and have a meal in one of the front rooms that has an enormous fireplace and would be cosy in cold weather. As we drove back to the cottage I took notes on all that Maria had shown me, with the intention of including them in my 'hidden treasures' talk.

Work progressed steadily on the extension and we found the noise, dust and half-living in the caravan and half on the upper floor of the cottage to be uncomfortable. However, all of that was bearable next to the endless decisions that had to be made. Sometimes the builders would say that the architect's instructions in the plans were impossible to carry out. They would claim that the architect didn't know what he was talking about and that the work would have to be done differently.

Although Randy had worked in construction and was very good at DIY, he sometimes didn't know enough to decide if the builders were, in fact, trying to get away with short cuts to suit them or if they were correct and the architect had made a mistake. The strain of trying to sort this out was becoming very stressful.

After a couple of months, the work, although going more slowly than planned and of course costing more than anticipated, was showing some good results.

The piggery hadn't fallen down and, after the walls were secured with metal braces, it was complete, with the exception of a section of roof tiles. The cottage was now joined up with the cart shed and the piggery and the windows were in along with some of the flooring. The electrics were in place and the plastering had been started.

Randy had also made quite a few trips to various reclamation yards and had bought reclaimed pine doors, door handles, hinges, bathroom fixtures, all great bargains, storing them well wrapped up in plastic in the garden under several tarpaulins

Randy had been able to pitch in, doing a fair amount of work on the cottage and had also somehow managed to record an entire season of his cartoon series.

There was never a dull moment with the building and we seemed to ricochet from one set of problems to another. Our project manager Fred had done a good job, until a family crisis meant he was absent part of the time and finally had to leave the job altogether. Randy decided to take over to save on costs and Fred gave him all his information before he left, so this was a big help. But it was still an organisational headache. Fortunately, The Listed Property Owners' Club and the members that Randy networked with for advice were a tremendous help.

Next, there was a flurry of site meetings with Mr A, the conservation officer and a building regulations officer. At times the latter two could not agree on how things should be done. Mr A was an amazing diplomat and eventually everything got sorted out.

Sometimes our problems were truly bizarre. One day, a builder was stung by a wasp, had an allergic reaction and went into shock. He was alright in the end but there were a few scary moments before emergency services arrived. The ambulance man was a wag and, after he had treated the builder, said, "When I saw the builder's lorry outside the cottage I thought the home owners had keeled over with shock because they'd just been given the bill."

This joke was too near the truth for us, as a recent accounting had shown that we were teetering on a tightrope with our finances. If nothing more went wrong and we could keep on track with more work coming in we could just squeak by, before the filming had to start and Randy's family arrived from America for their Christmas visit. Of course, we would still have a lot of debt to pay off eventually.

Both of us were run ragged with juggling all this. We were almost at the end of our tether when we received an invitation from our friends Pat and William.

These friends were the couple that I had written about in my last book, *Cotswolds Memoir*, who had visited when we all took a trip on the Thames. I described an eventful boat ride when, due to a thunder storm, I ended up wearing a cup of tea on my head. Now we were invited to stay in their villa in Provence over a bank holiday weekend.

We jumped at the chance. The builders would not be working because of the holiday so we found a deal on air tickets to Marseille and booked them.

Just as we were packing to leave, a letter arrived from the film company to say the location filming at the cottage was proceeding earlier than originally planned.

Included in the letter was a paragraph copied from my contract with them that showed I had agreed to this should it become a possibility. There it was in the fine print.

I hadn't given much thought to this when I read it originally as the window of time available had seemed so large at the beginning of our project. Now it was shrinking to nothing.

As I wailed, Randy, calm as ever, reminded me that there was nothing to be done at the moment, we were off for a few days of well-deserved holiday so we may as well enjoy ourselves.

I am the worrying kind, however, and wondered how we could make everything come out right with this new spanner in the works.

As I turned to the second page of the letter and read more, the film company stated the actual date they would be arriving.

"Look Randy," I said, "they want to start filming just before Christmas, the same time that your family is coming. Help, what are we going to do? The extension won't be finished in time for any of this!"

Nine

FOODIE DELIGHTS
Stroud, Duntisbourne Abbots, Frampton Mansell

"OUCH! I've been bitten!"

Our flight was delayed by a crew scheduling problem and by the time we reached our destination our friends had been waiting several hours to pick us up in Marseille. When we arrived we were actually asleep on our feet.

"We have to put you in the living room on a pull-out sofa," explained Pat as we headed towards the villa. "Sorry about that, another couple who are visiting were due to leave today but missed their flight – so no spare bedroom."

"Don't worry – we'll be fine," I replied.

We sank gratefully on to our makeshift bed, in front of the fireplace in the living room and fell asleep in seconds.

Sometime later from the depths of a dream I heard a buzzing noise, followed by a moaning sound.

"Ohh, I've been bitten again." Randy was sitting bolt upright, clasping his hand.

A second buzzing sound was added to the first and another and another.

We fumbled around to turn on a light which illuminated dozens of large hornets flying down the chimney and into the room. Waving a newspaper only agitated them further. Not wanting to disturb our friends upstairs I tried to repress squeals of fear as the scene turned into a horror movie. More hornets were filling the air by the second.

Randy hurriedly folded our bed back into a sofa and we dragged it, with loud scuffling and clanking noises, across into the kitchen. It was extremely heavy and we were panting loudly by the time we got it there. Quite a few hornets got into the kitchen with us before we could shut the door. Randy found some insect spray while I hid under a sheet. He sprayed, but this enraged the hornets further. One of them got under the sheet and buzzed into my face.

"Oh... it's so big!" I screamed involuntarily.

"And getting bigger!" yelled Randy in alarm.

"Get off me!" I screamed.

I suddenly noticed Randy's hand – the bites on his finger had made it twice its normal size.

"Look, it's swelling... it's enormous!" I exclaimed. Another hornet attacked me.

"I'm going to hit it with a newspaper!" I yelled, as I struggled to get away.

By now we had made so much noise that there was no way anyone could still be asleep upstairs. But we didn't hear a sound. While we didn't want to disturb our friends, we felt somewhat mystified as to why nobody had come to help. But there was silence except for the buzzing of the hornets and our occasional screams.

Finally, a cautious voice said, "Need any help?"

Apparently, Pat, William and the others had misinterpreted my cries of, "It's swelling... it's enormous," and, "I'm going to hit it with a newspaper."

All the sounds we'd made had been mistaken for the two of us having a frisky night between the sheets!

Before finding out what had really happened, Pat and William had wondered which vitamins we took that made us that frisky after the exhaustion generated by working on the cottage and a long-delayed flight. There was a lot of laughter when we explained our problem with the hornet's nest.

Our friends created a big blaze in the fireplace and this put paid to the hornets and Randy iced his hand. The next morning we breakfasted on croissant chocolat and latte and followed this with a swim in the pool. We lounged in sun chairs and caught up with everybody's news. As we chatted, Pat and William wanted to know about our latest explorations in the Cotswolds.

We described our recent trip to Stroud, which had begun when Randy needed a special DIY tool that he had located there. Our visit had evolved into an immensely enjoyable outing.

We went on a Saturday as it was the farmer's market on that day and to shop at its organic food stall, which was reputed to have a huge variety of fruit and vegetables. We were surprised by how much we enjoyed Stroud's vibrant, slightly bohemian, bustling market day scene. The stalls, grouped all higgledy-piggledy around the high street, are an eclectic collection of food, clothing and vintage finds. There are a number of interesting specialty shops of all kinds and a vintage trail, highlighting the many antique, nostalgia and rare book shops of Stroud. I had grabbed a map for this trail from the Tourist Information Office and found that several of the antique and vintage shops listed were right where the market stalls were located. However, Vintage Mary, whose stall is well-known in these parts for a range of kitchen items and linens was, to my disappointment, only there on a Friday. After a good rummage around we were ready for coffee and a snack and found the terrific J. Rool Bistro in a quiet alley away from the noise of the bustling market. We pegged it for a return visit around lunch time, as the dishes that were going by our table looked delicious. Next, we strolled around the town a little, which is hilly and has lovely views. We didn't stay long, but made a note to return soon, as there were more visits to make.

On our way out of the market we shopped at the organic stall, which was even better than described and headed next for The Malt House, an excellent antiques emporium a few minutes' car ride out of Stroud. I did a whistle-stop tour of the six-thousand square feet of floor space in record time and bought a very inexpensive antique mirror that would be perfect for the living room in the extension.

Our next stop, a few miles away, was in the pretty village of Duntisbourne Abbots in Gloucestershire and on my list to explore. I had not visited this part of the Cotswolds at all and it turned out to be a revelation. This small village is breathtakingly beautiful, with a collection of ancient cottages grouped on hilly terrain around the 12th century St. Peter's Church. There were photo opportunities galore, and in searching for a better view we almost came to grief at the point of crossing a shallow ford only to find that this was actually the River Dunt!

Luckily, we had stopped in time as we were warned of the danger by a friendly local who also gave us directions to a good pub for lunch. He directed us to the next village, Frampton Mansell, singing the praises of its pub. As we drove through the village and approached the Crown Inn, a glorious vista unfolded before us. The inn overlooks 'The Golden Valley', as it was aptly named by Queen Victoria when she rode on a train through this gorgeous countryside. This is the Frome Valley and The Crown Inn's outdoor tables were ideally situated on the prow of a hill to view the lush greenery descending to the valley floor below, with rolling, tree-covered hills rising above in the far distance on the other side.

The Crown Inn was built in 1633 and the front bars appear untouched since then. It is wonderful to see such an authentic pub that has not been gentrified. Meanwhile, in the back, everything is neat as a new pin with a modern dining room situated in the conservatory.

It was a gorgeously sunny day and I was thrilled to sit overlooking the lovely view and be served a delicious meal of fresh seafood stew for lunch.

I was in Cotswold heaven, with the perfect pub, great food and oh... that view.

Pat and William were particularly interested in the Crown Inn and we made a tentative date to get together there once we were all back in England and the extension was finished.

I also filled Pat and William in on my latest publicity coup. I was really pleased to have been approached by the stylish, foodie magazine, *Crumbs*, whose editor got in touch after seeing my site on Twitter, and requested an interview featuring my book *Cotswolds Memoir* and focusing on its foodie aspects.

As the lavender in the front garden was in full bloom, and had not been trodden down by the builders, I made this herb the theme of my dishes and drinks.

I had prepared Cotswold Lavender Lamb, a boneless leg baked in a Cotswold honey glaze infused with lavender. I had talked the builders into temporarily hooking up the electricity to the oven in the kitchen especially to do this. Everything else I managed in the caravan kitchen.

I had previously made a pitcher of lemonade from organic lemons sweetened with Cotswold honey. Separately, I made an infusion of lavender, and when the *Crumbs* team arrived, suggested that everybody 'watch the magic'. Next, I poured the infusion into the lemonade and enjoyed the oohhs and ahhhs as it turned from pale yellow to a glowing lavender.

I did a set-up for high tea and afternoon tea combined and served Cotswold devilled eggs on a kitsch egg plate I had found at Church Westcote village fete for £2.00.

On a tier cake plate I had piled cupcakes covered with lavender coloured icing and served everything on fine bone china with silver cutlery picked up from village fetes and antique fairs. Then I used a mixture of Ceylon and Lapsang Souchong leaves for the tea, which blended perfectly with the lavender.

The friendly and talented *Crumbs* team stayed quite a while, interviewing me in a relaxed manner, obligingly taking dozens of photographs in little vignettes that did not include the construction on the extension. They stayed late enough for me to offer them a Lavender Gin Fizz.

Randy had suggested pouring some left over lavender infusion, from making the lavender lemonade, into ice trays to freeze for use at a later date. This produced lavender coloured ice cubes and gave me the idea of creating a Gin Fizz cocktail in which these featured.

In a cocktail shaker I added a mixture of lavender syrup, gin and elderflower cordial, and after giving it a good shake I poured it into elegant cocktail glasses.

The lavender ice cubes, several sprigs of fresh lavender and a few frozen purple grapes were used for decoration. The lavender ice cubes looked wonderful in this drink and added a delicate fragrance. The recipe for Lavender Lemonade and Gin Fizz appears as a blog post on my website DizWhite.com.

During the interview and photo shoot one of the questions posed was about the kind of food my mother had cooked for me as a child when we were on picnics or outings.

I told Pat and William that I tried to come up with one of those 'magazine answers', describing haute cuisine dishes that my mother had cooked to develop my palette at a young age. But, instead, I had an instant flashback from an outing that occurred during my 'colourful' childhood that most likely would not have been included in a publication of this kind. As Pat and I go way back she laughed in anticipation of what was to come.

This flashback transported me to one of my family's weekly outings, in which food was prominently featured, a trip to the Saturday morning pictures. My mother, brother and I were sometimes accompanied by our Auntie Vi and her two children (who were even bigger rascals than me and my brother). We four kids were thrilled to be watching the films but Mum and Auntie Vi saw this as an opportunity to get out of the house and catch up on gossip.

We would stagger to the cinema under the weight of a week's worth of provisions, carrying several paper carrier bags, a couple of wicker picnic hampers and a small suitcase containing a Thermos flask and half a dozen cups. We lugged it all through the rows of cinema seats till we found a place to sit. Often as not it would be raining and Auntie Vi would invariably drop her umbrella, which had a habit of springing open, as we pushed past the unruly children, showering them with cold rainwater and causing shouts of protest.

Once we had settled down, steam would rise from our clothes as Mum dug out piles of ham and cheddar cheese sandwiches, a small mountain of chicken drumsticks, bags of crisps, a jar of pickled onions, another of pickled walnuts, several whole beetroots, three or four fruit and nut chocolate bars and a dozen oranges. She would then produce a jumbo-sized Thermos, precariously balance plastic cups on the arms of the seats and pour molten-hot cocoa into them before shoving this lot into our greedy little hands.

We managed to devour all this despite having our eyes glued to the images in front of us as a manic cartoon short filled the screen. If there was any food left after we had stuffed ourselves to bursting point, we would start a food fight with the other kids in the cinema. Instead of reprimanding us, Mum and Auntie Vi would settle in for their gossip and merely duck to miss the half-eaten sandwiches and orange peel that flew over their heads.

Before long, Auntie Vi would bring out her knitting. This was an elaborate affair with several sets of needles hanging off of various corners. This garment always seemed to be a large, half-finished Fair Isle cardigan with an incredibly complicated pattern that involved four or five different coloured balls of wool. She would gossip on, never stopping to draw breath, her fingers flying as she frenetically clicked and clacked away in the darkness, without ever dropping a stitch. However, she frequently lost control of her balls of wool as she pulled at them to free up more of the yarn. This would often send the balls of wool rolling away under the cinema's seats accompanied by her shrieks of dismay.

It was our job to retrieve them and this added to the mayhem as we pushed through the crowded rows of seats disturbing everyone.

"Gimme my Auntie's wool – it's down there. Pass it under the seat will ya?"

We kids saw the opportunity for mischief as we did this and would deliberately make a bad job of it. Before long, half the kids in the cinema would be tangled up in knots and Auntie Vi would be screaming for her wool not to be broken.

On one occasion my brother sneaked our little mongrel dog into the cinema under his coat and released it at the height of all this madness. It ran about joyfully under the seats, barking loudly at all the fun and causing even more havoc as it dodged the ushers and tangled Auntie Vi's wool into a Gordion knot.

This uproar was often drowned out as the main movie began, its volume always twice as loud as the cartoon that preceded it. The film's racket thundered through the cinema, but Mum and Auntie Vi never paid the least bit of attention to it. They just raised their voices to a shout, managing to be heard above the cowboy and Indian battles raging in front of them. Sometimes I would listen to them instead of the movie.

"So how's your Alfie these days?" asked Mum.

"Oh just the same," replied Auntie Vi.

Mum tut tutted. "He never lets you alone does he?"

"No, he'll never change," sighed Auntie Vi. "Mind you, nowadays I'll only let him have it once every couple of months."

"How does he let you get away with that then?" asked Mum.

Auntie Vi, yelling above the big finish on the screen of ear-splittingly loud gunfire and war whoops from the final battle replied, "He's got no choice now I've had the kids. As soon as he climbs on I say, 'Come on hurry up... what are you doing down there?'"

Needless to say, I did not relay this flashback from my childhood to the interviewer for *Crumbs* magazine and managed to come up with a suitable answer.

I had brought the copy of *Crumbs* to show Pat, William and our friends and as we flicked through it and looked at all the food photos I was glad we were cooking right then.

Pat and William were preparing delicious salt-crusted dorade and it was so relaxing to sit in the surprisingly warm air, as it was fairly late in the year, at the massive granite table on the villa's terrace as the dorade cooked in one of those fish cages on the barbeque. Pat enclosed the whole dorade (also known as gilt-head bream) in a mixture of salt and egg white after stuffing it with fresh fennel. Their villa is near Aix-en-Provence and the local specialties include walnuts, walnut oil and virgin olive oil. Another specialty was the locally produced rosé, which magically never seemed to make me tipsy. Pat prepared a salad of tender butter lettuce with whole walnuts and walnut oil and aged Balsamic velouté for the dressing. To this was added slices of avocado and finally a big dollop of sour cream and some crumbled St. Agur cheese. This was a delicious accompaniment to the fish which was served on a bed of cous cous, with more of that lovely rose wine.

All too soon the few days in Provence whizzed by. We had caught up on our news, gossip and sleep, eaten delicious French food, put paid to more than a few bottles of wine and had lots of laughs with our friends.

We left, however, with a visible reminder of our visit as Randy jokingly waved goodbye with his swollen, hornet-stung hand. This produced gusts of laughter, reminding everyone of the misunderstood non-frisky night under the sheets.

It was time to get back to all the problems of the extension. I had managed to stop worrying for a few days but now it felt like returning to pushing a boulder up a hill. But at least we felt more refreshed as we arrived back in England.

Ten

COTSWOLD BLISS
Warwick, Broughton, Beveston

"Oh no… this can't be…what's happened?"

Back at the cottage we discovered what seemed like total devastation. While we were away we had been burgled and, worse, vandalised as well. All of Randy's carefully chosen reclaimed pine doors, hardware for them and bathroom fixtures were gone, along with some new roof tiles for the piggery, which wasn't quite finished, and other building materials. Hose pipes had been turned on and most of the new building work was flooded. One hose pipe had been thrown against a wall and an enormous wet patch was spreading across it.

I started shaking. I couldn't see any way we could overcome this setback in time to meet all our commitments for Christmas. We had already spent the loan I had secured against the film location rental, to say nothing of where we would accommodate Randy's family if the renovation wasn't finished in time

It was especially sad as on the plane coming back from France we had gone over our finances and worked out that if nothing more went wrong we could just about make it with covering the cost of the extension.

Now it looked like we were sunk.

We called the police.

"Thieves have been known to follow people home, who are doing renovation work, from a building supplier or a reclamation yard," one of the officers said. "Then they bide their time and wait for an occasion like a bank holiday when, most likely, nobody will be in the home or on the site."

This may have been the case with us. But they were now long gone.

Randy seemed really defeated. All that time and money spent at the reclamation yards. We had home owner's insurance on the cottage for theft – but I knew the paperwork required would delay payment. We were really up against it and I saw bankruptcy looming in our future.

The builders were sympathetic and we begged them to put a spurt on to finish in time for the filming. But the cottage had to dry out before a lot of the work could continue. We all mopped and swabbed and when the excess water was cleared out rented some dehumidifiers to help get rid of the damp.

Once the damp was gone, Randy carried on doing his best alongside the builders. In between jobs he started the discouraging task of gathering all the reclaimed building materials all over again. Fortunately, the builders put out a call to all their contacts and more supplies of the roof tiles were located fairly quickly. Now we had to pay for them before the insurance money reached us.

Desperate for some work, I took a long shot and contacted a magazine in Hong Kong that paid well, to propose an article. I knew that many of the Asian visitors to the Cotswolds were fascinated by castles and fortified buildings in the area. I proposed to write an article about three Cotswold castles.

Thankfully, my proposal was accepted. I negotiated a fee and set to work. I began with a research trip to Warwickshire on the very outer reaches of the Cotswolds.

There was not much traffic. so before long I reached the outer northern reaches of the Cotswolds and found myself staring into the eyes of the squire of Warwick Castle depicted in a portrait, hanging in the Great Gallery there from 1628, and as I did a shiver ran through me. His gaze seemed to follow me as goose bumps prickled my spine, for this was the famous painting of Sir Fulke Greville whose ghost, it is said, frequently terrifies startled visitors as it often suddenly materialises out of his portrait and haunts the castle to this day.

The stern-looking Sir Greville, wearing an Elizabethan ruff and a strange Tyrolean-like hat, met his maker in dramatic fashion at the hands of his servant, and as a result haunts the Watergate Tower (now known as the Ghost Tower) of the castle and has been seen emerging from his portrait on a number of occasions throughout the centuries. This servant, Ralph Haywood, after years of faithful service, discovered that the unkind, stingy Fulke Greville had not mentioned him in his will. Finding he was to be left nary a farthing, poor old Haywood snapped, stabbed his master and then in a fit of remorse did away with himself too.

This is one of many gory stories, my research showed, from the 1,000 year plus history of Warwick Castle, which today is an amazing mixture of fascinating history and a sort of family theme park. The castle is now owned by the Madame Tussauds' Group and their expertise has been applied to the clever recreations and re-enactments that bring history alive to the delight of the teeming visitors who swarm over it almost every day of the year.

Throughout its long and tumultuous history, Warwick Castle has seen more than its share of momentous events. A history that includes war, mayhem and the making of kings.

William the Conqueror ordered the construction of Warwick Castle to fend off the invading Danish Vikings, and its ancient walls provided an impenetrable barrier to their armies. Later, other armies pitted all their forces against these monolithic walls without result. Murder holes situated over the entrance of the castle were used by the defenders of this fortress to pour boiling oil on their enemies below. These murder holes were also a convenient place from which to shoot arrows down upon the marauding hordes.

After fleeing from Sir Greville's creepy portrait, I climbed up on to the ramparts of the castle to see the spectacular views of the Avon and the surrounding countryside. The crenelated battlements that line the roof of the castle were not decorative but meant to provide shelter to protect archers. Later, as Britain became less barbaric, fortified manor houses gradually replaced castles and these eventually gave way to mansions and finally stately homes. I clambered around, exploring various turrets and towers, finally descending into the scary castle dungeons, the setting of countless beheadings, tortures, murders and stabbings some of which were recreated by actors in an impressive performance. In one such event in 1312, the first of Earl of Cornwall, Piers Gaveston was captured by the 10th Earl of Warwick, Guy de Beauchamp, and imprisoned in this dungeon. He was beheaded later that year.

It was something of a relief from the earlier barbaric history of the castle to find in another section superbly recreated settings for the very civilized Royal weekend parties that were held during late Victorian times and attended by some of the most important personalities of that era.

In the first room I encountered a mannequin of Edward, Prince of Wales, who was a frequent visitor to the castle, and is shown together with another figure of Lord Curzon, Viceroy of India. I had recently indulged in the guilty pleasure of reading *Dirty Bertie: An English King Made in France* by Stephen Clarke that chronicles Edward, The Prince of Wales' love life. Wicked and witty as this book is, it still manages to get across the fact that the prince, the original architect of entente cordiale, was a terrific diplomat. I photographed these two historic figures who looked as if they had stepped right out of Victorian times.

One of the Royal bedrooms in this wing displayed a mannequin of Frances 'Daisy' Greville, the Countess of Warwick. Although married to Francis Greville, whose title was Lord Brooke, she was also the mistress of Edward, the Prince of Wales. Lady Brooke, as she was also known, was notoriously indiscreet and gossiped constantly about her affair with the future King. News of this quickly spread around London at that time and as a result she became known as 'the Babbling Brook'. She is the Daisy who inspired the famous music hall tune *A Bicycle Built for Two*.

I knew my Asian readers would also like to hear about the Great Hall, the state rooms and the landscaped gardens, with their sculptured topiary peacocks and fragrant Victorian rose garden.

In the grounds it was exciting to watch the formidable siege machine, the trebuchet, in action. This is a reconstruction of a huge catapult, which in medieval times hurled rocks and stones in an effort to breach castle walls.

Finally, I was fascinated to learn that it is now possible to book accommodation in the castle's 14th century Caesar's Tower and a narrow, circular staircase of 70 steps leads to the Peacock and Rose suites. Included is a private, expert-led castle tour. After all the day visitors leave, red ropes are drawn aside and hidden rooms are opened up to reveal the servants' quarters which feature, among other attractions, graffiti written by Civil War prisoners. Guests are invited to try on armour, mock fence with 500-year-old swords and to examine ancient tapestries. It would be wonderful to stay there, even if Sir Greville's ghost might make things go bump in the night. Warwick Castle has it all and is a rewarding place to visit, especially if there are kids in tow.

Next, I visited the nearby lively small town of Warwick. Once fortified, it was largely destroyed in 1694 in the Great Fire of Warwick and most of the buildings post-date this event. The east and west gatehouses still survive from the burning. 'Warwick' means 'dwellings by the weir'.

I wrote up the section about Warwick Castle and moved on to Oxfordshire.

Beautiful Broughton Castle is defended by a moat and appears to almost float in the reflection of the water surrounding it. Built in the year 1300 by Sir John de Broughton it is situated on the junction of three streams and is two miles from Banbury.

More of a medieval manor house than a castle, it was enlarged in the 16th century and is the home of the Fiennes family, Lords Saye and Sele. Many medieval rooms survive, in addition to a whole suite of remarkably intact Elizabethan interiors. James I slept in the King's chamber. However, there was no damage to the castle in the Civil War. Viewers of the television show *Wolf Hall* may recognise this lovely building as one of its settings. I was amazed to discover that the ownership of the Broughton Castle has remained in the same family since 1447.

Finally, I visited the tiny unaltered village of Beverston, which is two miles west of Tetbury in Gloucestershire and is home to Beverston Castle, dating from the 12th century. Much of this building is in ruins but the section still standing is now a residence. I call this the cosy Cotswold castle as it is small and friendly compared to Warwick or Broughton. Maurice de Gaunt built the original castle and it has gone through a number of building stages since then. Much of the castle was destroyed in the Civil War but what remains is extremely interesting. It is surrounded by a pretty garden and well worth a visit.

I quickly finished the article on the three castles and sent it off, asking to be paid as soon as possible.

Now it was back to the race against time to get the cottage finished.

Things were not looking good. There was so much to be done.

The film company was proposing to come shortly before Christmas and the builders predicted that the extension would be finished in early January.

I came out in a nervous rash and Randy looked haggard. I looked up bankruptcy on the Internet to see how long it would take to dig ourselves out if it. Seven years seemed the shortest estimate.

First, I decided to call the film production company, as I didn't want to let them down at the last minute and to tell them that the cottage would be unavailable for filming. I had no idea how we were going to repay the loan.

There was static on the line when I got through to the Chuck, the location manager, in Los Angeles but I could just hear him. Before I could speak my piece, however, he said with a southern drawl.

"Did you get my message?"

"No," I said, "what was it?"

"I thought you didn't. The email bounced back. I know you were expecting us to start filming just before

Christmas, well you know what the movie business is like – the schedule has changed and now we want to come a couple of weeks after Christmas instead," he said. The line crackled.

"What did you say?" I said, since I thought I was dreaming.

"We are coming after Christmas now. Hope that doesn't mess you up. I know you put it in your calendar and here we are changing on you."

I let out a whoop of joy.

"What was that?" asked the location manager.

"Oh... eh... I don't know, there's a lot of static on the line. Eh... no that's fine."

"Great. We'll firm up the actual date as soon as possible," he said.

Whew! I almost fainted with relief when I got off the phone. One crisis averted, one more to go. If only we could finish enough of the extension for it to be functional for Randy's family to stay, we could get through. All I needed was to be able to cook in the kitchen, have the living room ready and for the central heating to be back on. If this could be accomplished a couple of days before Christmas then I could manage. Although I had been turning out meals for the builders in the caravan kitchen, I knew I wouldn't be able to cook Christmas dinner there.

But could it be done? When friends, family and friendly neighbours heard what a fix we were in they rallied round. Everybody was wonderful and really pitched in. The Murgatroyds sent over their jack of all trades, handyman Pilkins, who was unintelligible but very competent at all kinds of things. His country accent was so thick that Randy communicated with him in sign language and drawings. Another neighbour was a licensed electrician, which was great, as the subcontractor that the builder was using to work on our cottage was also working another renovation and couldn't be available for some of the time. A friend who is an interior designer sent a couple of his employees over and the builder brought in more men.

The racket of the hammering and all else was tremendous, but there was also a great energy. The race against time was making the goal of finishing the project a competition and the fever for a desire to win was catching. The builders seemed to work faster and take shorter tea breaks and when they left for the day our friends took over.

On one particular night we had about a dozen people over helping with a variety of jobs. Everybody worked very hard until I served a late dinner.

My caravan kitchen was too small for me to produce a meal for this crowd so we sent out for a curry. As we enjoyed our meal the chatter inevitably turned to show business because there were a number of actors among our friends. We were talking about the fun of doing voice work when Dan, one of our neighbours, asked a question.

"How long have you been able to project your voice so you could be heard at the back of a theatre?"

"Since I was born," I replied.

"Really?" he asked doubtfully,

"Yes," I replied, "true story. Two days after I was born the doctor came to my mother's hospital bed and asked her if she wouldn't mind leaving as soon as possible. When my mother asked why, he said, 'Because your daughter's voice is so loud it is disturbing all the other babies.'"

More showbiz stories followed and my friend Susan talked about the time she had been a starving drama student and performing in a show at the Edinburgh Festival.

All sorts of venues serve as performing spaces during the festival and Susan was acting in a fast-moving sketch comedy show in a freezing cold, run-down legion hall. It was discovered that an artistic director of a big theatre was coming to the evening's performance and if he liked what he saw would book the sketch comedy show in his theatre's studio space. This could be the actors' big break. But the legion hall was so cold that a performer's breath was clearly visible on stage. Despite the festival being held in August it is often excruciatingly cold in

Edinburgh and the actors decided that the theatre had to be warm or the director might not stay for the entire performance. This led to a desperate solution, with the actors performing a farce both off stage and on. During the show, every actor not involved in a sketch that was currently being performed on stage would tear down stairs to the basement, chop up a chair or any other available furniture and throw it in the wood burning furnace. Then this actor would fling himself or herself back up the stairs and make it, often with only seconds to spare, back on stage for the next sketch. These manic antics continued throughout the show, and although the actors collapsed in an exhausted heap, at the end it was worth it – the director booked the show.

But I think my favourite was a contribution by Dave, one of our actor friends who had just watched a rerun of *Absolutely Fabulous*. Seeing June Whitfield playing the mum on this show reminded him of a passage in her autobiography entitled *And June Whitfield*. He recounted June's story about Rex Harrison, one of the stars of *My Fair Lady* and numerous other films.

"This was in the heyday of the matinee tea, an unusually disruptive custom whereby theatregoers were able to order and consume a full tray of tea, scones and cakes without stirring from the comfort of their seats. It was supposedly served in the interval, but often lingered through the second and third acts. Rex Harrison was once giving a performance when someone in the front row placed their laden tray on the front of the stage. Rex strolled elegantly towards it, poured himself a cup of tea and scoffed their cakes."

After a few more stories we called it a night, with everybody still laughing as they made their way home.

It had been an unusually mild winter until suddenly the weather turned and our jobs were made harder by the bone-chilling cold coming from the Arctic. By now the extension was getting closer to being finished but we still didn't have the heating back on.

To sleep we had moved into the small guest room upstairs, as it was easier to keep warm than the top floor with the master bedroom. I had bought half a dozen hot water bottles to ward off the cold. These, two space heaters and every sleeping bag we had piled on the bed just about prevented us from freezing.

In the middle of one of these freezing nights, which was now accompanied by snow, the phone rang. I blearily fumbled for my cell phone.

"Gee," said Chuck the location manager, "did I wake you? Sorry, lost track of the time difference. The director wants to come before Christmas after all. Apologies for this. Just wanted to let you know and I assume that is OK with you?"

Suddenly, I was wide awake. This wasn't a horror movie, it was really happening. My heart started beating very fast and I trembled with visions of bankruptcy floating before my eyes.

"Well em... I'm not sure," I stuttered, trying to come up with a stalling tactic. "I'm having a bit of decorating done since you had postponed the shoot."

"Oh that's OK," Chuck replied, "the director looked at your weather forecast over there and as it is going to snow he only wanted some B roll exterior shots."

"Ohhh....that's no problem," I said, with a huge sigh of relief. Phew, another close shave.

Randy was so tired he had barely woken up but I trembled for another half an hour before I got back to sleep. Wow, the ups and downs – would I survive? What next, I thought as I drifted off.

The 'what next' came soon enough when the heating engineer phoned to say he wasn't coming to get the central heating back on because his van was snowed in. We were now only a few days away from our cut-off date, which was to be the day before Christmas Eve when Randy's family were due to arrive.

I was in despair. Everything else was, by now, looking like we could just maybe make it. My fee had arrived from the magazine article and Randy had received his cartoon series payment and some unexpected rerun money besides. This would tide us over for the immediate bills.

The builders were working flat out on the kitchen floor and the living room and although there would still be quite a bit to do, having these two rooms functional and the heat on would get us through Christmas.

Now this latest drama threatened everything. We tried phoning around to get someone else to deal with the central heating, but being so close to the holidays it was impossible. Several engineers said they would do it – after Christmas.

We couldn't quite understand what the problem was with the engineer, although there was snow about we could still drive around without difficulty. It turned out that this engineer was coming from the Stow-on-the-Wold area which is the highest point in the Cotswolds and unshielded from the icy winds, so there was a lot more snow up there.

Randy had an idea. He found out where the engineer was located and very resourcefully took a big snow shovel and some boards and went off to try and dig him out.

Next, I got a phone call from the film company to say that the plan had changed *yet again*. The bad weather was causing too many delays and the B roll exterior filming of the cottage in the snow would be delayed until after Christmas. It almost beggared belief that the film company had changed their plans again but I was so happy they had. As I was sighing with relief over this, Randy called to say he had succeeded in digging out the heating engineer's van and they were on their way. I took this as a good omen and then it suddenly dawned on me that we might really be able to have a Christmas after all.

Thoughts flashed through my mind of when Randy and I had a fantasy about spending Christmas in our little cottage in the Cotswolds.

At the time, foodies that we are, we had slipped into an overindulgent gourmet reverie of all the foods we would cook in our cottage if we ever managed to find one.

I talked about dishes I wanted to make from old Victorian recipes passed down to me through several generations of my family.

In our fantasy we imagined some of the possibilities, which included beef suet pudding, steamed with nutmeg and Worcestershire sauce, jugged hare casseroled in red wine and cloves, kedgeree made with salmon and pickled walnuts, roasted goose and pease pudding, quail with truffles and wassail punch.

"What about dessert?" asked Randy.

"Hmm, let's see... I know, Nesselrode pudding, spotted dick, trifle cake with brandied cherries and chestnut soufflé."

By the time Christmas Day arrived, the heating engineer had the central heating going and the builders, together with all our friends, had come through for us, bless them all. There was a lot still left to finish off in the piggery and the new bathroom but, except for a few bits of woodwork in the living room, the cottage was ready just as we hoped on the day before Christmas Eve!

As I thanked the builders and our friends I couldn't help having a bit of a blub, but not for long as next there was a frantic rush to get ready for Christmas Day.

It had been a close-run thing. A taxi dropped off Randy's mother, sister and a couple of cousins and as they walked down the garden path they passed the builders going the other way, carrying their tools.

Randy's family were charmed with the cottage and we took them to the upstairs bedrooms as Randy and I were now camping out in the unfinished dining room that had previously been our postage stamp living room.

As the family unpacked and took their jet-lag naps, Randy and I worked at warp speed to furnish the living room. One of the builders had helped Randy earlier to carry in our sofa, which my sister had generously given me after she remodelled her living room. I now placed the early 19th century tilt table, that I had risked my life for in the Bric-a-Brac Dash, at the end of this. On top of it I placed a pretty Victorian table lamp and a couple of silver framed pictures. A few weeks earlier I had found an almost new set of brocade curtains at a Sue Ryder shop, which fitted perfectly when Randy placed the brackets for the curtain poles at just the right height. Next, we filled the alcove by the Inglenook fireplace with logs and piled more of them into a big basket on the hearth. On the other side of the fireplace I placed my early find from Portobello Road Market, a Thonet bent wood and cane rocking chair, which looked just right. I threw down some soft rugs and several crushed velvet cushions on the sofa and onto an old leather armchair we had found at an antique fair. Randy had managed to get a few bookshelves up earlier, on which I placed some leather-bound books, framed by book ends of carved wooden elephants. We brought in two or more Victorian spoon back chairs, bought from Witney Warehouse, on which I draped patchwork crocheted throws, and placed an old pine coffee table in front of the sofa.

We had borrowed a trestle dining table and mismatched dining chairs from the village hall which Randy positioned at one end of the room. I had bought a new red sheet which I threw over the table and tied red bows on the chairs.

Some friends had been shopping for a tree and had bought an extra one for us. To decorate it they had thoughtfully included several sets of fairy lights with red bulbs. I saved a few sets of lights for the window frames and the top of the vintage mirror, now above the fireplace, which had been bought in the Malt House after our trip to Stroud. I had no ornaments for the tree so I dashed around the cottage grabbing everything red I could find, including red silk roses from my sunhat, a pair of Randy's red socks, red reels of thread, all my red jewellery, some Christmas cards decorated with red glitter and the red sparkly crackers we were to pull after lunch. The result was much better than I expected and passed for a new look in ornaments. A large holly tree on our land was covered in red berries and Randy cut down a bunch of branches from it and these made wonderful Christmas decorations. They handily covered up a few unfinished bits of woodwork and made the living room very festive.

Randy got a log fire going as I lit candles and we stood back and admired our work. Perhaps it was because we were decorating a room that was built in the 17th century, with its one-foot thick walls and old beams, that everything blended in so well. The room appeared to have been lived in for years and looked extraordinarily comfortable and inviting.

On Christmas Eve, the Murgatroyds came over for a drink, and as their children were away skiing and they were spending a quiet Christmas, we insisted upon them staying for dinner. We all had such a good time that nobody noticed several inches of snow silently drifting down as the evening wore on. By the time the Murgatroyds were ready to leave it would have been too much to dig out their car. So they stayed the night and we put them where we had been sleeping in the unfinished dining room. Randy and I waded through the snow to the caravan, took out all the recording equipment and slept there with every hot water bottle we could find, all the sleeping bags and Fudge the neighbour's cat.

On Christmas morning, the Murgatroyd's car was completely snowed in along with the rest of the village. Everything was under a gorgeous, deep blanket of snow. Ice crystals sparkled everywhere and there was that muffled silence that comes with a lot of snow. The Murgatroyds had no alternative but to stay, and as my family had to cancel, because it was impossible to drive into the village, it was no problem to have them join us for Christmas lunch.

I had managed to get in a whirlwind shopping trip with my pen pal Maria a couple of days before Christmas and got everything I needed in the way of food.

This meant that on Christmas Day Randy and I were able to make our fantasy Christmas a reality.

Lunch was unbelievably cosy, served by the Christmas tree as the log fire crackled in the grate. And straight out of my fantasies Randy and I cooked a roasted goose with a sage and onion dressing and a port wine sauce. Added to this were roast potatoes, sweet potatoes, parsnips, Brussels sprouts and pease pudding. And, of course, even though they normally don't go together, I had to have my big puffy Yorkshire puddings made with a little goose fat. For dessert there was Duke of Cumberland pudding cooked with suet, apples and nutmeg.

There were lots of laughs and fun pulling crackers and exchanging gifts. I had not had the time or money to buy proper gifts so instead on my shopping trip for the Christmas lunch ingredients I had dashed to a party shop in Witney and bought a big pile of false noses, bunny ears, silly glasses, pig masks and fake moustaches. I wrapped them all individually in red tissue paper, put them in a basket and offered them all to my guests as a lucky dip. This grab bag was the hit of the day, as everybody looked so ridiculous wearing them. Even the Murgatroyds were laughing and this loosened them up enough for me to get Mrs M to relate one of her old stories. It took a little coaxing but finally she talked about the time, near the end of the war, when she was very young and daring. She had lied about her age to be able to join the Voluntary Aid Dispatch. She had no training as a nurse but managed to get the authorities to let her join as a cook to help the war effort.

"After working there for several months I had a day's leave and I went with another gal to the Cheltenham Horse Trails," she said. "There was no petrol so we had to hitch-hike. We got several lifts and then, when we were close to Cheltenham, by lucky chance, a Duke who was a friend of Daddy's picked us up. He was going to the horse trails too and when we all arrived he insisted we join him for the day. We hadn't realized that he'd been invited by King George and Queen Elizabeth. We were introduced to them and stayed in their company the entire time. We couldn't believe our luck. When it was time to leave we set off to hitch-hike back again, however the Duke wouldn't hear of it.

"'Just a moment,' he said, 'I'm going to ask the King if you can stay in Windsor Castle, a good deal of it is closed up so I want to make sure there is room.' It turned out there was and before we knew it we were whisked off in a Royal car and taken to the only turret in Windsor Castle that had not been closed up because of the war. This was where the entire Royal Family was living for the time being. We didn't have any night things with us, so on our arrival Princess Elizabeth and Princess Margaret rushed around the castle looking for spare nighties and toothbrushes. They were so kind." Mrs M paused, making sure she had everyone's attention. "It's not often a gal can say that the Queen of England was once her lady's maid."

Everybody was mesmerized by this story and persuaded Mrs M to tell several more.

After this, it was time for afternoon tea, which was served with a flaming Christmas pudding, brandy butter and vanilla ice cream.

We also served sack posset, an old-fashioned eggnog made with milk, nutmeg and Madeira. Hilariously silly charades followed and then some spirited, if off-key, carol singing. When everybody ran out of puff we played a video of Randy from the spring, shortly after our arrival in the Cotswolds. This showed Randy as he tried to scare away the cows when they threatened to ruin our garden. I explained that when nothing else worked Randy sang *Come to the Cabaret* and added some of Fosse's choreography. As Randy performed his deranged dance on the screen the expression on the cows' faces caused gales of laughter from everybody, and when the cows turned as one and galloped off the laughter doubled.

The video recalled the warmth of that April, with its drifts of brilliant daffodils and other budding blossoms. It was a lovely reminder that the promise of a new spring, while still a little way off, was on its way.

Next, we showed an old movie, and soon several of our guests nodded off to sleep.

In a short while our living room resembled a scene from Dylan Thomas's *A Child's Christmas in Wales*; after the big feast everybody gets warm and fuzzy by the log fire and some of the uncles fall asleep and snore a little.

Randy came over, snuggled up with me on the sofa and draped Fudge on top of our feet. Fudge had come over on the hunt for leftovers and, having had his fill, now obligingly curled up on our furry Christmas slippers, making our toes toasty and warm. We sat there, listening to the cat's soft purr, gazing at all our guests and the cosy cottage scene with deep contentment.

"Well," whispered Randy, "who would have thought that this would be an even bigger roller coaster ride than buying the cottage?"

"Not me," I said.

"Do you think it's been worth it, this time too?" he asked.

"Oh yes," I replied, "despite all the ups and down. The mad things we've done to stretch the money, teetering on the edge of bankruptcy, the shock of the planning permission being turned down, the collapsing piggery, pretending to be French to get a job in Hollywood, the hornets' stings, the film company zigging and zagging, all the help from our wonderful family and friends, finding the Listed Property Owners' Club when all seemed lost, yes, it really has been crazy."

We sat reflecting on all this, as the logs murmured in the fireplace and gave off a rosy, warm glow.

Randy handed me a glass of Champagne, we clinked glasses and took a sip.

"Now all we have to do," I said, "is remake the garden after the builders have ruined it and, of course, get through the filming."

"Uh ohh. I don't know what made me think we were done," said Randy. "When will I learn? Will this be yet another Toad's Wild Ride?"

"Who knows," I smiled. "But what if it is? You know it doesn't get much better than this. How could it? We are in Cotswold bliss."

More Cotswolds Memoirs

Visitor Guide

Here is an eclectic guide, by no means comprehensive, which represents my choices of the crème de la crème of inns, attractions and activities culled from over ten years of research. A number of these entries describe little-known gems from the off-the-beaten track Cotswolds that are well worth a visit.

BONUS

This guide includes the postcode for instant input in GPS or Sat Navs (often hard to find even on official websites) for all entries, plus a web address for more in-depth inquiries.

PLEASE NOTE

Visitors would be wise to check opening times and days of all activities before setting forth.

Official tourist websites, resource guide and conservation information are at the end of this Visitor Guide.

Readers. Any suggestions to add to the Visitor Guide would be very welcome. Contact me at:

Dizwhite.com or on Twitter – @dizwhite

ACCOMMODATION, RESTAURANTS, PUBS, TEA ROOMS

THE BELL AT SAPPERTON,
Sapperton, GL7 6LE
www.bellsapperton.co.uk
Good pub food. Bustling.

THE CAT AND CUSTARD POT,
Shipton Moyne, Gloucestershire, GL8 8PN
www.catandcustardpot.co.uk
Good pub food. Like the name.

THE CORNER CUPBOARD,
Winchcombe, Gloucestershire, GL54 5LX
www.cornercupboardwinchcombe.co.uk
Built 1550. Close to Sudeley. Restaurant serves all day.

COTSWOLDS DISTILLERY,
Shipston-on-Stour, Warwickshire, CV36 5HG
www.cotswoldsdistillery.com
Lovely setting. Visit for great whiskey/gin tastings.

COTSWOLD VILLAGE ROOMS,
www.cotswoldvillagerooms.co.uk
Pre-selected, charming B&B rooms. Great value.

THE CROWN INN,
Frampton Mansell, Gloucestershire GL6 8JG
www.thecrowninn-cotswolds.co.uk
View Golden Valley. Outstanding food. Rustic.

EDGEMOOR INN,
Near Painswick, Gloucestershire, GL6 6ND
www.edgemoor-inn.com
Spectacular views. Cotswold Way. Great food and beer.

THE FALKLAND ARMS,
Great Tew, Chipping Norton, Oxfordshire, OX7 4DB
www.falklandarms.co.uk
Rustic Gastropub Rooms with 4-poster beds. Got it all.

THE FEATHERED NEST,
Nether Westcote, Oxfordshire, OX7 6SD
www.thefeatherednestinn.co.uk
Gorgeous views. Outstanding, upscale food. The best.

THE FOX AT ODDINGTON,
Near Moreton-in-Marsh, Gloucestershire, GL56 0UR
www.foxinn.net
Charming, cosy inn. Fine food. Lovely patio.

THE FUZZY DUCK,
Armscote, Warwickshire, CV37 8DD
www.fuzzyduckarmscote.com
B&B in Shakespeare country.

THE GREEDY GOOSE,
Chastleton, Gloucestershire, GL56 0SP
www.thegreedygoosemoreton.co.uk
Modern, peppy. British favourites.

HE SAYS SHE WAFFLES,
Cirencester, Gloucestershire, GL7 2AA
www.hesaysshewaffles.co.uk
Freshly-made comfort food. Outdoor seating. Yummy!

THE HORSE AND GROOM,
Bourton-on-the-Hill, Gloucestershire, GL56 9AQ
www.horseandgroom.info
01386 700413
Outstanding fine food. Pub of the Year. Don't miss.

JOLLY NICE,
Frampton Mansell, Gloucestershire, GL6 8HZ
www.harrietsjollynice.co.uk
Exceptional homemade cakes. Some organic vegetables.

THE LADY JANE TEA ROOM,
Winchcombe, Gloucestershire, GL54 5HT
www.theladyjanetearoom.co.uk
Elegant. Fine cakes made on premises. Patio.

LE MANOIR AUX QUAT'SAISONS,
Great Milton, Oxfordshire, OX44 7PD
www.manoir.com
Raymond Blanc's restaurant. Need deep pockets.
Sublime.

LOWER SLAUGHTER MANOR,
Lower Slaughter, Gloucestershire, GL54 2HP
www.lowerslaughter.co.uk
Croquet on lawn. Fine or casual food. Elegant manor.

MADE BY BOB,
Cirencester GL7 2NY
www.foodmadebybob.com
Fun. Bustling. Good Food.

THE OLD SPOTTED COW,
Marston Meysey, Wiltshire, SN6 6LQ
www.theoldspottedcow.co.uk
Rustic pretty pub. Good pub food.

THE PLOUGH INN,
Kelmscott, Gloucestershire, GL7 3HG
www.theploughinnkelmscott.com
Fine food. By the Thames. Pretty garden.

THE POTTING SHED PUB,
Crudwell, Malmesbury, Wiltshire, SN16 9EW
www.thepottingshedpub.com
Lovely old gastro-pub. Excellent fine food.

THE PRIORY CAFÉ,
Burford, Oxfordshire, OX18 4QA
www.prioryrestaurantburford.co.uk
Great breakfast/lunch only. Pretty patio.

PRITHVI,
Cheltenham, Gloucestershire, GL53 7HG
www.prithvirestaurant.com
Great fine dining Indian style. Excellent service.

THE ROSE AND CROWN,
Shilton, Oxfordshire, OX18 4AB
www.roseandcrownshilton.com
Outstanding food. Pretty, rustic pub.

THE ROYAL OAK,
Bishopstone, Wiltshire, SN6 8PL
Organic meat. Very rustic pub.

SHERBORNE VILLAGE SHOP & TEA ROOM,
Sherborne, Gloucestershire, GL54 3DH
www.sherbornevillageshop.com
Charming cottage tea room, tea on front lawn.

THE SNOOTY MEHMAN,
Littleworth, Oxfordshire, SN7 8PW
www.snootymehmaan.com
Excellent upscale Indian dining.

SOHO FARMHOUSE,
Great Tew, Oxfordshire, OX7 4JS
www.sohofarmhouse.com
Deep pockets needed. Excellent rooms.

THE SWAN AT SOUTHROP,
Southrop, Gloucestershire, GL7 3NU
www.theswanatsouthrop.co.uk
Top gastro-pub. Rooms in Southrop Estate.

THE SWAN INN,
Swinbrook, Oxfordshire, 0X18 4DY
www.theswanswinbrook.co.uk
Mitford pub. Great inn. Chickens in garden.

TROUT AT TADPOLE BRIDGE,
Faringdon, Oxfordshire, SN7 8RF
www.trout-inn.co.uk
On Thames. Fine dining. Six rooms. Boat moorings.

THE TUNNEL HOUSE INN AND BARN,
Cirencester, Gloucestershire, GL7 6PW
www.tunnelhouse.com
Pub food. Camping in the grounds. No rooms.

THE VILLAGE PUB,
Barnsley, Gloucestershire, GL75EF
www.thevillagepub.co.uk
Charming gastro-pub. Lovely village.

WILD GARLIC,
Nailsworth, Gloucestershire, GL6 0DB
www.wild-garlic.co.uk
Elegant, fine dining.

THE WINDMILL CARVERY,
Nr. Burford, Oxfordshire, 0X18 4HJ
www.windmillcarvery.co.uk
Good food. Great value. Go back for seconds.

WINSTONES,
Stroud, Gloucestershire, GL56 0SP
www.winstonesicecream.co.uk
Now have ice cream parlour. Serves tea/coffee.

WOEFULDANE ORGANIC DAIRY,
Minchinhampton, Gloucestershire, GL56 0SP
www.woefuldanedairy.co.uk
Charming, excellent deli and tea room.

THE WOOLPACK,
Slad, Gloucestershire, GL6 7QA
www.thewoolpackinn-slad.com
Laurie Lee's favourite pub. Good food. Lovely valley.

ANTIQUES

GRIFFIN MILL ANTIQUES EMPORIUM,
Thrupp, Gloucestershire, GL5 2AZ
www.antiquesgriffinmill.co.uk
Affordable vintage furniture.

COTSWOLD HOME & GARDEN,
www.cotswoldhomeandgarden.co.uk
Upscale. Great finds.

THE MALT HOUSE EMPORIUM,
Stroud, Gloucestershire, GL6 6NU
www.malthouseemporium.com
6,000 sq ft of vintage finds.

SCUMBLE GOOSIE (Reproduction Antiques),
Thrupp, Gloucestershire, GL5 2AZ
www.scumblegoosie.co.uk
New fine furniture.

STATION MILL ANTIQUES,
Chipping Norton, Oxfordshire, OX7 5HX
www.stationmill.com
Two floors of vintage & antiques.

WITNEY WAREHOUSE,
Witney, Oxfordshire, OX29 7EY
www.witneywarehouse.com
Vintage and new stylish furniture.

BARNS

ASHLEWORTH TITHE BARN,
Ashleworth, Gloucestershire, GL19 4JA
www.nationaltrust.org.uk
National Trust. Built 1481-1515. By the River Severn.

GREAT COXWELL BARN,
Faringdon, Oxfordshire SN7 7LZ
www.nationaltrust.org.uk/great-coxwell-barn
Outstanding example of medieval craftsmanship.

BOATING

COTSWOLD BOAT HIRE,
Lechlade, Gloucestershire, GL7 3HA
www.cotswoldboat.co.uk
Day cruisers and small boats for the River Thames.

COTSWOLD COUNTRY PARK AND BEACH,
Cirencester, Gloucestershire, GL7 6DF
www.cotswoldcountrypark.co.uk
Pedal boats and row boats on a lake. Family fun.

CASTLES

BERKELEY CASTLE,
Berkeley, Gloucestershire, GL13 9BQ
www.berkeley-castle.com
Outstanding 12th century Norman fortress.

BROUGHTON CASTLE,
Banbury, Oxfordshire, OX15 5EB
www.broughtoncastle.com
Beautiful 'small' castle.

SUDELEY CASTLE,
Winchcombe, Gloucestershire, GL54 5JD
www.sudeleycastle.co.uk
Once home of Henry VIII's wife. Family fun.

WARWICK CASTLE,
Warwick, Warwickshire, CV34 4QU
www.warwick-castle.com
1,000 years of history. Great for kids. Has it all.

CHURCHES

ADDERBURY,
St Mary the Virgin, Adderbury, Oxfordshire, OX17 3LP
www.adderbury-stmarys.com
Most important in Oxfordshire. 12th century.

ST.KENELM'S CHURCH,
Church Enstone, Oxfordshire, OX7 4NN
Pretty, remote. Enstone home of 'Old Mont'.

ST. GEORGE'S CHURCH,
Kelmscott, Oxfordshire, GL7 3HG
www.oxfordshirecotswolds.org
Red ochre wall paintings from 1280.

ST. PETER'S CHURCH,
Winchcombe, Gloucestershire, GL54 5LU
www.pjohnp.me.uk/winchcombe.htm
Famous for grotesques, gargoyles and more.

FARMS

THE BUTTS FARM,
South Cerney, Cirencester, Gloucestershire, GL7 5QE
www.thebuttsfarmshop.com
Great for kids. Check for times. Terrific shop too.

COGGES FARM,
Witney, Oxfordshire, OX28 3LA
www.cogges.org.uk
Downton Abbey filmed here. Great for kids.

COTSWOLDS FARM PARK,
Nr. Guiting Power, Gloucestershire, GL54 5UG
www.cotswoldfarmpark.co.uk
Rare breeds. Camping. Family fun.

FOOD SHOPPING

THE BUTTS FARM SHOP,
South Cerney, Cirencester, Gloucestershire, GL7 5QE
www.thebuttsfarmshop.com
Terrific shop. Meat bought by 10,000 a year.

CUTLER AND BAYLISS,
Lechlade, Gloucestershire, GL7 3AX
www.cutlerandbayliss.co.uk
Simply the best.

DAYLESFORD FARMSHOP & CAFÉ,
Near Kingham, Gloucestershire, GL56 0YG
www.daylesfordorganic.com
Deep pockets needed but worth it. Farm tours.

GARDENS AND ARBORETA

NATIONAL GARDEN SCHEME,
www.ngs.org.uk
Visit rarely seen private gardens.

BATSFORD ARBORETUM,
Moreton-in-Marsh, Gloucestershire, GL56 9AB
www.batsarb.co.uk
Once home of Mitfords. Deer park. Falconry centre.

HIDCOTE MANOR GARDEN,
Near Chipping Camden, Gloucestershire, GL55 6LR
www.nationaltrust.org.uk/hidcote
National Trust. Outstanding garden 'rooms'. Views.

HIGHGROVE HOUSE GARDEN (Prince Charles' home),
Near Tetbury, Gloucestershire, GL8 8PH
www.highgrovegardens.com
A thyme walk. Many garden rooms. Beautiful in June.

KIFTSGATE COURT GARDEN,
Near Chipping Camden, Gloucestershire, GL55 6LN
www.kiftsgate.co.uk
Close to Hidcote. Both in one day. Spectacular views.

PAINSWICK ROCOCO GARDEN,
Painswick, Gloucestershire, GL6 6TH
www.rococogarden.org.uk
Beautiful. Anniversary maze. Pan, God of Love.

WESTONBERT ARBORETUM,
Tetbury, Gloucestershire, GL8 8Q5
www.forestry.gov.uk
16,000 trees within 17 miles of paths.

MANOR HOUSES

BUSCOT PARK,
Faringdon, Oxfordshire, SN7 8BU
www.buscot-park.com
National Trust. Adam. 1780. Gorgeous gardens.

CHASTLETON HOUSE,
Near Moreton-in-Marsh, Oxfordshire, GL56 0SU
www.nationaltrust.org.uk
National Trust. Stuart manor. 1602. Long gallery.

CHAVENAGE HOUSE,
Near Tetbury, Gloucestershire, GL8 8XP
www.chavenage.com
Finest Tudor house in Britain. Visited by Cromwell.

KELMSCOTT MANOR,
Near Lechlade, Oxfordshire, GL7 3HJ
www.kelmscottmanor.org.uk
William Morris's home. Open two days a week.

MINSTER LOVELL HALL,
Near Witney, Oxfordshire, OX29 0RN
www.english-heritage.org.uk
12th century, picturesque ruin by Thames.

OWLPEN MANOR,
Owlpen, Dursley, Gloucestershire, GL11 5BZ
www.owlpen.com
Romantic Tudor manor house. Group visits.

RODMARTON MANOR,
Near Cirencester, Gloucestershire, GL7 6PF
www.rodmarton-manor.co.uk
Arts and crafts. Elegant gardens.

SNOWSHILL MANOR,
Broadway, Gloucestershire, WR12 7JU
www.nationaltrust.org.uk
National Trust. Charles Wade's collection. Organic garden.

UPTON HOUSE,
Near Banbury, Oxfordshire, OX15 6HT
www.nationaltrust.org.uk
Smaller country home. Built 1695. Fine furniture.

WOODCHESTER MANSION,
Nr. Stroud, Gloucestershire, GL10 3TS
www.woodchestermansion.org.uk
Victorian Gothic. Unfinished. Strange, haunted.

PREHISTORIC SITES

BELAS KNAP LONG BARROW,
Winchcombe, Gloucestershire
www.english-heritage.org.uk
Neolithic long barrow. 1400 BCE. Excavated in 1863.

ROLLRIGHT STONES,
Nr Chipping Norton, Oxfordshire/Warwickshire border
www.rollrightstones.co.uk
Neolithic stone circles. 2500 BCE.

RAILWAY

GLOUCESTER AND WARWICKSHIRE RAILWAY,
Toddington, Gloucestershire, GL54 5DT
www.gwsr.com
Runs through Cotswolds. Termini with huge engines.

ROMAN SETTLEMENTS

CHEDWORTH ROMAN VILLA,
Yanworth, Cheltenham, Gloucestershire, GL54 3LJ
www.nationaltrust.org.uk/chedworth-roman-villa
Roman villas. 4th century mosaics. Museum. Family fun.

NORTH LEIGH ROMAN VILLA,
Witney, Oxfordshire, OX29 8ER
www.thecotswoldgateway.co.uk
Remains of Roman Villa. 60 rooms. Mosaic floors. Free.

VIEWS

BROADWAY TOWER,
Middle Hill, Broadway, Worcestershire, WR12 7LB
www.broadwaytower.co.uk
Folly built 1798. Spectacular views of dozen counties.

CLEEVE HILL,
Nr. Cheltenham, Gloucestershire
(See website for directions) www.cheltenham4u.co.uk
Views over Prestbury, Cheltenham & Severn Vale.

DEVIL'S CHIMNEY,
Leckhampton Hill, Near Cheltenham, Gloucestershire
(See website for directions) www.cheltenham4u.co.uk
Local landmark. Views across Cheltenham.

HARESFIELD BEACON,
3 miles north west of Stroud (see website for directions)
www.gloucestershire.gov.uk
National Trust. Spectacular views. Hill fort.

RURAL SKILLS

THE LLOYD-BAKER COLLECTION OF RURAL LIFE,
The Old Prison, Northleach, Gloucestershire, GL54 3JH
Rural skills demonstrated. Contact for schedule.

COTSWOLD WOOLLEN WEAVERS,
Filkins, Gloucestershire, GL7 3JJ
www.dspace.dial.pipex.com/town/plaza/hk67/
18th century working woollen mill.

COTSWOLD DRY STONE WALL CLASSES,
www.thecotswoldgateway.co.uk
Learn how to build a dry stone wall. Declining in the
Cotswolds. Carry on tradition.

WILDLIFE

COTSWOLDS WILDLIFE PARK,
Near Burford, Oxfordshire, OX18 4JP
www.cotswoldwildlifepark.co.uk
Lions, zebras. 160 acres of parkland. Family fun.

COTSWOLD FALCONRY CENTRE,
Batsford Park, Moreton-in-Marsh, GL56 9QB
www.cotswold-falconry.co.uk
Huge variety. falcon displays. Great for the kids, too.

Tourist Information Centres and Info

There are 20 Tourist Information Centres in the Cotswolds. Access all through:

COTSWOLDS TOURIST INFO

www.cotswolds.info
www.the-cotswolds.org
www.escapetothecotswolds.org.uk

COTSWOLDS CONSERVATION

COTSWOLD CONSERVATION BOARD,

www.cotswoldsaonb.org.uk
The Cotswolds Conservation Board exists to conserve and enhance the Cotswolds Area of Outstanding Natural Beauty (AONB).

SOCIETY FOR THE PROTECTION OF ANCIENT BUILDINGS,

www.spab.org.uk
SPAB fights to save historic and listed buildings from demolition and destruction.

NATIONAL TRUST,

www.nationaltrust.org.uk
Pay membership and then no fee for castles, stately homes, gardens and more.

COTSWOLDS FARMERS MARKETS

PRODUCE AND FARMERS MARKETS,

www.cotswold-produce-and-farmers-markets
www.thecotswoldgateway.co.uk

COTSWOLDS FÊTES, EVENTS, COUNTY SHOWS ETC.

Search these links for information regarding these Cotswolds events:

www.events.wiltsglosstandard.co.uk
www.stowonthewold.info/cotswold_village_fetes.php
www.oxfordshirecotswolds.org/whats-on
www.cotswolds.com/whats-on

WYCHWOOD FOREST FAIR,
Chipping Norton, Oxfordshire, OX7 4EU
www.wychwoodproject.org/cms/content/wychwood-forest-fair

MORETON SHOW,
Moreton-in-Marsh, Gloucestershire, GL56 0JQ
www.moretonshow.co.uk

COTSWOLD SHOW,
Cirencester, Gloucestershire, GL7 2BU
www.cotswoldshow.co.uk

Resource Guide

FOR LISTED HOME OWNERS or those embarking on renovation of old buildings

LISTED PROPERTY OWNERS' CLUB,
Lower Dane, Hartlip, Kent, ME9 7TE
www.lpoc.co.uk
Britain's only members' club dedicated to helping and advising listed buildings owners. Guidance on VAT, insurance, grants, loans, plus specialist suppliers and more.

BURGESS RECLAMATION,
Souldern, Bicester, Oxfordshire, OX27 7HT
www.burgessreclamation.co.uk

THE COTSWOLD RECLAMATION CO. LTD,
Little Rissington, Gloucestershire, GL54 2NF
www.cotswoldreclamation.com

PEEL AWAY,
www.dumondchemicals.com/home-peel-away-1.html
Non-polluting wood & moulding stripper.

RELICS OF WITNEY,
www.relicsofwitney.co.uk
Reproduction antique hardware.

WINCHCOMBE RECLAMATION,
Winchcombe, Gloucestershire, GL54 5NT
www.winchcombereclamation.co.uk

Ordnance Survey Maps of The Cotswolds

These 5 Ordnance Survey maps will help you plan Cotswold hikes across the entire Cotswold region:

OL45 – Stowe-on-the-Wold, Chipping Campden & Burford
179 – Gloucester, Cheltenham & Stroud
168 – Stroud, Tetbury & Malmesbury
191 – Banbury, Bicester & Chipping Norton
169 – Cirencester & Swindon

Maps may be purchased here
www.ordnancesurvey.co.uk

Books Referred to in
More Cotswolds Memoirs

The Pursuit of Love by Nancy Mitford
Hons and Rebs by Jessica Mitford
Lifting the Latch by Sheila Stewart.
The Mad Boy, Lord Berners, My Grandmother and Me by Sofka Zinovieff
Madresfield: One House. One Family. One Thousand Years by Jane Mulvagh
A Naturalist in Western China by Ernest Wilson
Dirty Birtie: An English King Made in France by Stephen Clarke
And June Whitfield by June Whitfield
Brideshead Revisited by Evelyn Waugh

Acknowledgements

I thank with all my heart the people who have made this book possible.

They include: Graham Cook and his great team; my lovely sister Linda, who inspired this book; Wanda Ventham and Tim Carlton, Coral Oswald and her family. Also, I thank Vivian Matalon, Gil Tobon, Katie Jarvis, Susan Bradley, Sally Landsberg, Jason Lavitt, Joe Perrotti, Mariette Vandermolen, Richard Kemp, Andrew Pywell, Bo Potter and Dr Claire Bland for all their help.

Gratitude goes as well to my dear pen pal and friend Maria, for her help, support and enthusiasm for sharing her extensive off-the-beaten-track knowledge of the Cotswolds. I wish also to thank James Wildman for his wonderful photographs and the Listed Property Owners' Club for their help and advice.

And most of all... I thank my dear husband and clever, patient helpmate, Randall Montgomery. His terrific photographic, graphic, editing and computer expertise do so much to enhance this book. In addition, his loving encouragement and willingness to put up with me through all the stages of getting this book to print were above and beyond.

Thanks too must go to all the lovely folks in my Cotswold village who have not only helped me in so many ways but have welcomed me into their community

Finally, I thank all the inhabitants of the Cotswolds, surely the most beautiful place on earth, who gave me their stories, hospitality and warmth during the wonderful adventure of writing this book.

Index

Bampton 35
Bampton Shirt Race 38
Beveston 155
Beveston Castle 155
Bourton-on-the-Hill 51
Broughton 155
Broughton Castle 154
Charlbury 112
Chevenage House 21
Chipping Campden 59
Church Enstone 111
Cleverly 114
Cogges 72
Cogges Manor Farm 73
Cogges Village 73
Cotswold Dry Stone Walling
    Academy 118
Cotswold Reclamation
    Yard 41
Coxwell Village 75
Crumbs Magazine 148
Dog & Duck Pub 37
Down Ampney 8
Downton Abbey
Film Locations in Cotswolds
35, 69, 72, 75, 76
Duntisbourne Abbots 143
Enstone 111
Enstone Fête 112
Ebrington 61
Fairford 11
Faringdon 132
Faringdon House 133
Frampton Mansell 144
Fulwell 111
Grantham Arms 37
Great Coxwell Barn 75
Hare in the Woods Deli,
    Faringdon 134

Heritage Day, Faringdon 134
Hetty Pegler's Tump 27
Horse & Groom Pub
    Bourton-on-the-Hill 54
Hugh Bonneville 76
Isobel Crawley's House 37
Kelmscott 177
Lady Edith 72
Listed Property Owners'
    Club 64, 183
Little Rissington 40
Lloyd Baker Rural Life
    Collection 119
Marigold 72
Mickleton 107
Minchinhampton 25
Minster Lovell 43
Mr Bates 76
Mummers 39
National Garden Scheme
Open Gardens 120
Neat Enstone 111
Newbridge 13
Northleach 120
Nympsfield 29
Owlpen Manor 29
Peel Away paint stripping
    product 47, 183
Prince of Wales 119
Priory Café, Burford 34
Prithvi Restaurant,
    Cheltenham 77
Red Lion Pub, Shilton 76
Rusty the Iron Age Man 56
Sezincote 52
Sezincote House 53
Shilton 76
Society for the Preservation
    of Ancient Junketing 38

St. Mary of the Virgin Church 36

St. Michael's of All Angels Church 36

St. Peter's Church Winchcombe 126

Stan the Station Cat 113

Standlake 138

Stanton Harcourt 137

Stowell Park Garden 120

Stroud 142

Sudeley Castle 127

Sudeley Village 128

Swinbrook 70

The Evenlode 103

The Feathered Nest Inn 103

The Lady Grey Tearoom, Winchcombe 125

The Pudding Club 107

The Ragged Cot 126

The Swan Inn, Swinbrook 69

Uley 127

Uley Bury 127

Uley Old Spot Ale 128

Upper Rissington 41

Warwick 154

Warwick Castle 151

Winchcombe 125

Winchcombe Imp 127

Winchcombe Reclamation 125

Wychwood Forest 103

Yanworth 121

Also by the author of this book:

Cotswolds Memoir*: Discovering a Beautiful Region of Britain on a Quest to Buy a 17th Century Cottage*

Available on **Amazon** in Paperback, Kindle and Audio Book

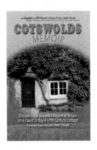

The story begins when British-born comedy actress Diz White realises that her roots are pulling her back from the glitz and glamour of Hollywood to Britain. The hunt is on to find her dream country cottage.

However, the search isn't just about finding the perfect house; it is about discovering the Cotswolds and meeting some wonderfully eccentric country characters along the way. Diz visits Roman settlements, Domesday churches, archeology digs, and enjoys river rambles, garden tours and pub walks.

During her search for a cottage, she is charged by a bull named Chasin' Mason, auditions for the hind end of a horse and is trampled by thirty children while wearing a bear suit.

There are laugh-out-loud moments, cliff-hanging twists and the satisfaction of a hard won prize. Not only is *Cotswolds Memoir* a wonderful story, it's also a valuable insight into some of the best 'off-the-beaten-track' Cotswold attractions and features a valuable Visitor Guide.

Diz enjoys hearing from her readers and can be contacted through her website **wwwDizWhite.com** or on **Twitter** @DizWhite.

PRINTED AND BOUND BY:
Copytech (UK) Limited trading as Printondemand-worldwide,
9 Culley Court, Bakewell Road, Orton Southgate. Peterborough, PE2 6XD,
United Kingdom.